SURVIVAL GUIDE FOR

A WEEKEND FATHER

P. Platt

ORCAS PRESS, INC.
Texas

Orcas Press, Inc. and Phyllis Platt assume no liability resulting from any errors or omissions in this book, or from the use of the information obtained herein.

Manufactured in the United States of America

Cover Artwork by Carolyn Hoefelmeyer

Library of Congress No. 87-60315
ISBN 0-9618546-0-X

This book is dedicated to Philip
- my husband and best friend

With special thanks to dear friends Sandra Schriever, Ellen Middleton, and Tom K. Low for helping make my wish a reality -- and to ALL of my children. They are my inspiration.

CONTENTS

INTRODUCTION

A period of time has passed since your separation or divorce and your life is finally starting to come back into focus. You are adjusting to your changing life and even to the reality of your divorce. Your job is beginning to make sense again and your co-workers are treating you more normally.

But, it is still very difficult to deal with your children. It feels strange seeing them only on an arranged schedule and not being at home with them. The children act as though they hardly know you. Conversation has become nods, grunts, and whining protestations. You are having trouble recalling that they are your children and that you love them. Making things even more awkward is the uncomfortable system of picking them up in front of your old home. (You find yourself wanting to drive away as quickly as the legal speed limit allows.) And now, that they are sitting in the car, what do you do with them? So far you have been to the movies twice, taken a car ride three times, and been to your mom's house six or seven times. You have taken the children to too many restaurants, and the food that was served was either too expensive, too fancy, or not nutritious enough.

You are beginning to realize that when the judge gave you visiting rights with your own children, he was asking you to assume the role of single-parent and not a gracious host. You are also becoming aware that parenting skills don't happen overnight.

Unlike your former wife, who started learning to be a parent when she was just a little girl playing "mommy" in the nursery school doll corner or baby sitting the neighbor's kids, you probably did not learn too many parenting skills and helpful household hints. Now you have to learn these skills quickly in order to enjoy the brief special times you have with your children.

SURVIVAL GUIDE FOR A WEEKEND FATHER has been written to introduce you to several aids, insights, and ideas, that will help you to enjoy your life with your children.

This volume includes two books. Book One of SURVIVAL GUIDE FOR A WEEKEND FATHER is called Going Places and Doing Things. Use this section of the book for ideas to help you plan a variety of activities. Make your weekend or vacation time together an adventure and a time for exploring and learning. Let the activities enhance your time together; don't use them for a barrier or an escape, and be sure to share quiet time.

Introduce yourself and your children to other people and other lifestyles. Help your children realize that although their family is changed and different, it is not less than it was.

You should try to learn about yourselves both as a special family and as individuals. Learn to listen and to hear. Make a point of discovering new ways of living. Learn to do ordinary house chores together. The children are going to be full of surprises, and you are going to be making changes in your life that are going to surprise them, too.

As a single father, you will be a different kind of parent. You will not be with the children all the time, but then neither are fathers who travel for business or who are in the armed forces. It is up to you to design your new life. It can work!

You will find yourself having to deal with the anger of your children, their hurts and the fears that are a result of the divorce, as well as your own pent-up emotions. There are going to be times that you will wish that you didn't have to pick them up from your ex-wife's house and there will be times when you won't be able to. You will find help in Book Two of SURVIVAL GUIDE FOR A WEEKEND FATHER. This section deals with these problems as well as others.

Not every part of this book will be relevant for every weekend father, but most will find some information or ideas in one section or another. You will find that this book can be a practical guide for establishing a weekend home for your children and for assisting you in coping with parenting. It has been designed with both you and your children in mind.

In summary:

- **Use the book as a source and a resource.**

- **Use it as an idea book.**

- **It explores places to go, vacations together, meals, and things to do.**

- **It lists over 365 ideas of places to go and things to do on weekends.**

- Use it for suggestions for living and places to live.
- It answers questions about housewares, clothing sizes and furniture needs.
- It discusses treating illnesses and how to handle emergencies.
- It talks about relationships with grandparents.
- It talks about relationships with friends.

BOOK ONE

Going Places and Doing Things

CONTENTS

BOOK ONE
Going Places and Doing Things

Chapter 3

Chapter 4

1

WHAT CAN WE DO? WHERE CAN WE GO?

Before your divorce, when you all lived together, everyone in your family had things to do or chores and responsibilities to take care of. Everyone's time was accounted for. In your new home, there are many differences in the way you live. Living in a home of your own means that in order for your kids to be with you, they have to be visitors.

At first, in this new environment the children don't have the chores, assignments, or friends that normally keep them busy. Therefore, because they feel a little like strangers and because they are not involved in familiar activities, you may find that the time you spend together ends up being a collection of awkward silences. You may end up having the feeling that you always must be doing something. The "Santa Clause Syndrome" appears-- you begin to feel that the only way you can keep the children's interest is to entertain them with movies, restaurants, trips, and gifts. It is at this point that many fathers, forced to choose between expensive entertaining or boredom, choose neither and start seeing less of their children.

It is not necessary to take such drastic steps, if you can make plans to live your life just as you did before. Make the chores, assignments, and small jobs involved in everyday living a part of your weekend and include the children. You can prevent dull weekends by planning activities that you can share and enjoy together. There are many activities that you can do at home or in your own neighborhood, and it is <u>not necessary</u> to go out <u>all</u> the time in order to entertain the children.

Because visitation commits fathers to a brief and specific time with their children, some fathers don't allow anything else to intrude on this time and, surprisingly, have found that they are learning more about their children and are spending more time with their children than they ever did before.

Make sure that the children are physically able to pursue any sports that you plan. Be aware that children of different ages must participate in activities differently.

You can get ideas of things to do and places to go from friends, libraries, church and synagogue bulletins, neighborhood newsletters, publicity posters in stores, scouts, youth groups, school publicity, airline magazines, Co-Op bulletins, travel agencies, state and city information offices, clubs and organizations, and so on. Start adding your own items of interest to the following list. Make a note when you hear of something that may seem like a good idea, even if you can't do it now. Write down things that might be of interest to you in the future, when the children are older or when you can better afford them.

Particularly, check your newspaper. Ideas will be found in the "Living," "Arts," "Leisure," or "Weekend" sections. There are also hints of activities mentioned in articles about people getting ready for special events like bazaars, art fairs, or community shows or benefits. Check news items, publicity items, and ads.

-+-

THE LIST OF PLACES TO GO AND THINGS TO DO

The following list of places to go and activities to participate in can help you start a list of your own. It is filled with ideas gleaned from all over the country. You may find that there are suggestions that are not necessarily appropriate to your geographic area, but you will find others that are exactly right.

The list is very general allowing you to interpret a suggestion so that it meets your own needs. For instance, the listing, "Paint a Picture" could be a reminder to build an easel so that you can do some poster painting, or perhaps try finger painting. It could start you thinking about painting a water color or learning about acrylic paints. Or perhaps you can do a velvet painting or take oil painting classes together at the neighborhood center. Note that whenever the word "you" appears it means you and your children. All of these activities are meant to be shared.

There is no particular order to this listing and frequently one suggestion just leads to another. There may be reminders of special local and professional events that you cannot attend this year, but in which you are interested. Make a pencil note of their performance date right next to the entry. Most professionally-sponsored events occur at the same time each year. Place a check or mark the date attended next to any events you do attend, and add a short comment. All the information that you can gather on an item will help you plan for events and things to do in the future. Planning in advance might even include deciding on taking a camera, packing a lunch, or choosing souvenirs for the Baby Book/People Book (see Chapter 9).

Some of the items and ideas on the list are for you and your children to do by yourselves. Some items are for participatory activities, and some you attend as spectators. Many of the items on the list are free while some have moderate costs. Others like professional events can be expensive. Make notes of entrance fees for the events you attend, or hope to attend, so that you can intelligently budget and plan for them.

In the next chapters of this book, many of these ideas will be explored further, with suggestions of how best to prepare for them.

The List

Date Attended	Event	Comments
	1. Zoo	
	2. Nature Reserve	
	3. Train Museum	
	4. Reconstructed Village	
	5. Wild Life Park	
	6. Planetarium	
	7. Fine Arts Museum	
	8. Sea World	
	9. Museum of History	
	10. Auto Museum	
	11. Air Show	
	12. Harbor	
	13. Hall of Fame	
	14. Sports Hall of Fame	
	15. Wax Museum	
	16. Aquarium	
	17. Airport	
	18. Train station	

Date Attended	Event	Comments
	19. Modern Art Museum	
	20. Animal Preserve	
	21. Science Museum	
	22. Nature Museum	
	23. Prairie Dog Park	
	24. American Indian Museum	
	25. Indian Reservation	
	26. Farm Machinery Museum	
	27. Auto Plant	
	28. Candy Factory	
	29. Country Fair	
	30. Amusement Park	
	31. Museum of Science/Industry	
	32. Seaport Museum	
	33. Old Sailing Ships	
	34. Museum of Industry	
	35. Fishing	
	36. Bike Riding	
	37. Tennis	
	38. Professional Baseball Game	
	39. Professional Football Game	
	40. Clamming	
	41. Swimming	
	42. Catching Frogs	
	43. Antique Airplanes	
	44. Museum of Black Americans	
	45. Boat Museum	
	46. Maple Sugaring House	
	47. Bake a Cake from Scratch	
	48. Glass Bottom Boat	
	49. Ferry trip	
	50. Top of a Skyscraper	
	51. Television Studio	
	52. Radio Station	
	53. Movie Studio	
	54. Space Center (NASA, Cape Kennedy)	

Date Attended	Event	Comments
	55. Space Launch	
	56. Fall Foliage	
	57. Sledding	
	58. Skiing	
	59. Pond Skating	
	60. Ice Rink Skating	
	61. Jai Alai	
	62. Horseback Riding	
	63. Apple Picking	
	64. Roller Skating	
	65. Amish Country	
	66. Camping	
	67. Climbing	
	68. Movies	
	69. Theater	
	70. Ballet	
	71. Children's Concert	
	72. Stamp Collecting	
	73. Coin Collecting	
	74. Shell Collecting	
	75. Building miniatures	
	76. Setting Up Trains	
	77. Radio Controlled Planes	
	78. Flying Kites	
	79. Touch Football	
	80. Circus Museum	
	81. Russian Museum	
	82. Old Fort	
	83. Polish Museum	
	84. Professional La Crosse Game	
	85. Professional Hockey Game	
	86. Doll and Toy Museum	
	87. Touch and Do Museum	
	88. Library Story Hour	
	89. Japanese Garden	
	90. Local Park	

Date Attended	Event	Comments
	91. Sail Toy Boats	
	92. Train Ride	
	93. Hot Air Balloon Show	
	94. Lighter than Air Show	
	95. Sailing	
	96. Windsurfing	
	97. Water Skiing	
	98. Playground	
	99. Picnic	
	100. Botanical Garden	
	101. Grange	
	102. Learn About Your Past--Weed a Family Plot	
	103. State Fair	
	104. Car Race	
	105. Glass Factory	
	106. Fish Cannery	
	107. German Museum	
	108. Other Ethnic Museums	
	109. Street Fair	
	110. Outdoor Art Show	
	111. Flea Market	
	112. Street Hockey	
	113. Ice Hockey	
	114. Hiking	
	115. Log Cabin Village	
	116. Whale Watch	
	117. Steel Plant	
	118. Aquacade	
	119. Ice Show	
	120. Theme Park	
	121. Play Ball	
	122. Water Slide	
	123. City Bus Tour	
	124. Watch Gymnasts	
	125. Tree Nursery	

Date Attended	Event	Comments

126. Children's Zoo
127. Attend a Church or Temple
128. Attend a Friend's Church or Temple
129. A Street Concert
130. Play Bocci
131. Checkers
132. Chess
133. Backgammon
134. Visit a Printer
135. Needlepoint
136. Paint a Picture
137. Create Clay Sculptures
138. Finish Pottery Greenware
139. Visit a Police Station
140. Visit a Fire Station
141. Play Cards
142. Play Horseshoes
143. Plant a Flowerbox
144. Plant a Tree
145. Plant a Garden
146. Adopt an Elderly Neighbor
147. Adopt a Shut-In
148. Visit a Fish Hatchery
149. Visit a Farm Zoo
150. Wind Surfing
151. Go To The Beach
152. Walk Across A Bridge
153. Visit an Animal Adoption Center
154. Circus
155. Frog Jumping Contest
156. Crewel Work
157. Visit Daddy's Office
158. Bazaars
159. Open Air Markets
160. Track Meet
161. Rodeo

Date Attended	Event	Comments
	162. Library	
	163. Football Training Camp	
	164. Baseball Training Camp	
	165. Treasure Hunt	
	166. Stamp Show	
	167. Rock and Gem Hunting	
	168. Ski Show	
	169. Dog Show	
	170. Cat Show	
	171. Gem Show	
	172. Dude Ranch	
	173. Archeological Dig	
	174. Dinosaur Tracks	
	175. American Landmarks	
	176. State Landmarks	
	177. Pigeon Show	
	178. Rabbit Show	
	179. Future Farmers of America Exhibits	
	180. Pet Show	
	181. President's Homes	
	182. Religious Settlements	
	183. Utopias	
	184. Film Festivals	
	185. Pageants	
	186. Renaissance Festivals	
	187. Shakespear Festivals	
	188. President's Libraries	
	189. Square/Round Dancing	
	190. Clog Dancing	
	191. Irish Fest	
	192. Polka Festival	
	193. Summer Opera	
	194. Jazz Festival	
	195. Craft Fairs	
	196. Magic Show	
	197. Carousel	

Date Attended	Event	Comments
	198. Folk Festivals	
	199. Visit Chinatown	
	200. Visit Little Italy	
	201. Visit a Magic Shop	
	202. Visit a Costume Shop	
	203. Make a Decoy	
	204. Watch a Parade	
	205. Craft Museum	
	206. Melon Festival	
	207. Watermelon Eating Contest	
	208. Water Gardens	
	209. Surfing	
	210. Kayaking	
	211. National Parks	
	212. Canoeing	
	213. Rafting	
	214. Wilderness Trip	
	215. Music and Light Shows	
	216. Panorama Movies	
	217. Tubing	
	218. Visit a Dam	
	219. Water Purification Plant	
	220. Arboretum	
	221. Miniature Golf	
	222. Mini Indy 500	
	223. Cross Country Skiing	
	224. Deep Sea Fishing	
	225. Sports Camp	
	226. Restored Towns	
	227. Backpacking	
	228. Berry Picking	
	229. Farm or Ranch Vacation	
	230. Visit a Canal	
	231. Visit a Reservoir	
	232. Build a Snowman	
	233. Sand Castle Building	

Date Attended	Event	Comments
	234. Visit a Lumber Mill	
	235. Visit a War Memorial	
	236. Visit a National Cemetery	
	237. Old Time Fiddling	
	238. Marching Band Festival	
	239. Mardi Gras	
	240. Alligator Farm	
	241. Armadillo Race	
	242. Snorkeling	
	243. Weave a Piece of Fabric	
	244. Make a Basket	
	245. Make an Igloo	
	246. Make a Tepee	
	247. Build a Dollhouse	
	248. Go to Clown School	
	249. Learn a Language	
	250. Start a New Collection	
	251. Attend a Sports Clinic	
	252. Collect Driftwood	
	253. Ice Boating	
	254. Play Scrabble	
	255. Play Chinese Checkers	
	256. Collect Wildflowers	
	257. Draw Wildflowers	
	258. Play Monopoly	
	259. Go on a Nature Walk	
	260. Practice Calligraphy	
	261. Try Liquid Embroidery	
	262. Sculpt	
	263. Make Candles	
	264. Play Horse Shoes	
	265. Learn About Computers	
	266. Arrange Flowers	
	267. Design a Bonsai Tree	
	268. Build a Go-Cart	

Date Attended	Event	Comments

269. Attend an Arts Festival
270. Go on a Picnic
271. Play with an Electronics Set
272. Go to a Puppet Show
273. Use a Chemistry Set
274. Be Helpers at a Special Olympics
275. Play With an Erector(R) or Lego(R) set
276. Make Marionettes
277. Work on Comic Book Collection
278. Make Macrame
279. Work on Cars
280. Attend Fireworks
281. Learn Archery
282. Collect Bugs
283. Go to a Snake Farm
284. Join a Choir Together
285. Go Scuba Diving
286. Jog
287. Attend a Wild West Show
288. Attend Pioneer Days
289. Play Badminton
290. Play Foosball
291. Knit
292. Woodworking
293. Metal Working
294. Do String Art
295. Make Bead Jewelry
296. Learn Indian Crafts
297. Lapidary Work
298. Tie-Dye
299. Make Stained-Glass
300. Feed the Ducks
301. Air Band Concert
302. Water Park
303. Mall Walk
304. Laser Show

Date Attended	Event	Comments
	305. Play Video Games	
	306. Go to the "Y"	
	307. Rock Concert	
	308. Wrestling Match	
	309. Dirt Biking	
	310. Photography Trip	
	311. Factory Tours	
	312. Cheerleading Clinic	
	313. Swimming	
	314. Diving Lessons	
	315. CPR Course	
	316. Lifesaving Course	
	317. Visit a Volcano	
	318. Indian Pow Wow	
	319. Boxing Match	
	320. Rowing	
	321. Visit a Nursing Home	
	322. Dune Buggy	
	323. Bird Watching	
	324. Neighborhood Park	
	325. Spelunking	
	326. Health Club	
	327. Ice Cream Factory	
	328. Gym	
	329. Drill Team Contest	
	330. Pony Rides	
	331. Greenhouse	
	332. Model Train Show	
	333. Tobogganing	
	334. Origami	
	335. Trolley Ride	
	336. Visit a Newspaper Office	
	337. Day Bus Trip	
	338. Day Boat Trip	
	339. Steel Smelter	
	340. Flower Festival	

Date Attended	Event	Comments

341. Soccer Match
342. Go to the Movies
343. Demolition Derby
344. Formula Racing
345. Throw A Frisbee
346. Start an Ant Farm
347. Visit an Astronomy Lab
348. Take a Mystery Bus Ride
349. Carve/Whittle
350. Dog Sledding
351. Take a Hayride
352. Take a Sleigh Ride
353. Dog/Frisbee Contest
354. Visit a Large Bread Bakery
355. Play Bumper Pool
356. Play Volley Ball
357. Go Bowling
358. Go to a Polo Match
359. Go to a Rugby Match
360. Build Balsa Wood Models
361. Chili Cookoff
362. Bargello
363. Coin Collecting
364. Latch Hook a Rug
365. Water Polo
366. Make Home Movies
367. Window Shopping
368. Put on a Muscular Dystrophy Carnival
369. Take an Air Boat Ride
370. Visit a Rattlesnake Farm
371. Learn to Use a Slide Rule
372. Learn to Read a Map
373. Go Orienteering
374. Make a Sundial
375. Mow the Yard
376. Mow a Neighbor's Yard

Add your own ideas to the list.

Date Attended	Event	Comments
	377. Run an Obstacle Course	
	378. Learn Carpentry	
	379. Practice Aerobics	
	380.	
	381.	
	382.	
	383.	
	384.	
	385.	
	386.	
	387.	
	388.	
	389.	
	390.	
	391.	
	392.	
	393.	
	394.	
	395.	
	396.	
	397.	
	398.	
	399.	
	400.	
	401.	
	402.	
	403.	
	404.	
	405.	
	406.	
	407.	
	408.	
	409.	
	410.	

2

PLACES AND PLANS

Question a group of people about why they find an activity to be fun, and their answers may surprise you. Some answers include: "Because --it was something that I never did before," or, "I always wanted to try that," or "It sounded interesting." Other answers might well be: "It's something new," "My friend tried it and liked it," or "I am good at doing such and so and this is more advanced." Others may say, "It looks like fun," or "I was bored and it was different." In each answer, they describe some aspect of learning, including gaining or improving a skill.

Most people seldom realize that learning is the basis for having fun. Learning takes place whenever one can see a difference in attitudes, and knowledge, or become able to deal with new information. In the home as in school, learning can be an important objective. The difference in interpretation between the home and school is in the formality of the approach.

Many of the activities that you plan for your weekend visits with your children can be learning experiences. But don't feel that you must plan them like classroom lessons. Be observant so that you will recognize that learning is taking place and then call upon that knowledge in other activities. Enjoy the newness of some activities and the familiarity of others.

The following group of 52 ideas for weekend plans is designed for two-day weekends. Use all of a suggestion or part of it. Combine it with other suggestions or use pieces of several. Like all the other parts of this book, this section is meant to be a guide and a help. If you see the children every other weekend, for one day a weekend, or even for only a few hours, use it in the way it fits your needs.

The very first thing to do is to join a public library. Get the children library cards. There is a book in the library for absolutely every activity you choose to do. Learn about an activity that you plan before you attempt it. You can prepare yourself with the answers to your children's questions before they ask them. Show your children how to look for sources for additional information. Many libraries have weekend and holiday activities for children ranging from story-telling hours to movies and marionette shows. Enjoy these activities, too.

Most of the following weekend plans include an item from the list in Chapter 1. These plans will include additional information on that item and on how to find where or how this activity takes place. A plan will include directions where appropriate, and what materials you may need to do it. The plans may also include a suggestion for books available on the subject.

When an activity is geared to a specific age group, or should be done differently by different age groups, that, too, will be noted.

-+-

Ideas for Fifty-Two Weekends

1
STAMP COLLECTING

Stamp collecting is an activity or hobby that everybody except the very youngest child can participate in. As a matter of fact, many grandparents enjoy this hobby with their grandchildren. A nine or ten year old may become a serious collector.

Stamp collecting usually refers to postage stamps, and you can start collecting those, using your own mail. Collect cancelled postage stamps from fellow employees, from friends, or buy stamps in bulk packages. Collections can be general or specific. Young children can start a collection of a certain type of picture (for instance, dog or flower stamps), regardless where they come from. Older children may want to collect themes from a chosen country or countries.

As your child becomes more involved with this hobby, he may show an interest in learning more about the methods of stamp production, perforations, watermarks, countries of the world, history, flags, and so on.

Start your kids off with a commercial stamp collecting book. Begin with an album that has illustrations that the children can match. However, don't expect illustrations for the most current postage. For a younger child, start with only a few stamps at a time so you don't overwhelm him.

Teach the child good stamp collecting habits, such as the use of stamp hinges or mounts, tongs, and possibly a magnifying glass. Use an informative catalog.

When you get stamps on an envelope, carefully cut around the stamp leaving some of the envelope. Save these stamps with a border of envelope until you have several. Follow the instructions that can be found in a stamp collecting book for soaking these envelope backs off the stamps.

There are many other things that you can do when a real interest in stamp collecting has developed. For instance, visit a stamp show when it is in town, or a store where stamps are sold. Go to a map store with the children or inspect a world atlas. Make or buy a map of the world and have the children find and mark the countries for which they have stamps.

If your children are interested, they may be able to get a pen pal in another country. Then, they will receive foreign stamps on their own personal mail. They may even be able to swap stamps.

The U.S. Post Office has an excellent publication (for sale) on stamp collecting which you can find out about in any post office. It is published frequently and brings information right up-to-date. Ask for the United States Postal Service "Stamps and Stories" Encyclopedia of U.S. stamps.

"Stamps and Stories" includes catalog numbers, denominations, descriptions, and pictures for stamps. The first day of issue catalog prices, quantity issued, and other information are also listed. This publication may require adult help in explaining terminology.

Other related books that you may find in the library include:

- "Getting Started in Stamp Collecting" by Burton Hobson
- "The International Guide to Stamps and Stamp Collecting" by Douglas and Mary Patrick
- "Beginning Stamp Collecting" by Bill Olcheski
- "Scott Standard Postage Stamp Catalogue"
- "Guide to the World of Stamp Collecting" by Viola Ilmad
- "Standard Handbook of Stamp Collecting" by Richard McP. Cabeen

Once the hobby of stamp collecting has begun, it can stay with a person all of his life. You will have enhanced your child's future, and perhaps added an interesting hobby to your own.

2
A TRIP TO THE ZOO

Almost everyone has taken his kids to the zoo at least once. Some folks swear never to do it again after the first trip. The usual situation that occurs is that everybody gets exhausted from all the walking, and still no one ever gets to see everything.

Plan a zoo trip that is carefully designed to eliminate all but a small area of the zoo. Be very specific and base the trip on the child's personal likes and dislikes.

All children that are old enough to voice an

opinion have a favorite animal. Most small children like monkeys, elephants, and other animals familiar from books and stories. Older children frequently have additional favorites. Make your plans a couple of weeks before you actually go to the zoo. Choose to visit only one or two of the animal varieties, and perhaps the "petting zoo."

Do some special things ahead of time to prepare for the zoo day and to get the children excited. During the week before you plan your trip, purchase animal cookie cutters, or cut animal shapes from cardboard. Buy some cookie dough (as suggested in the cooking chapter) and refrigerate it according to the package instructions.

Buy some animal picture books or borrow some from the library. If you can find books that are about the animals you are planning to see, so much the better. For instance, if you plan to visit the elephants, try to borrow a "Babar" book by Laurent or Jean de Brunhoff, or perhaps "Elephant Girl" by Ivor Cutler, or "An Elephant in My Bed" by Suzanne Klein. If monkeys are your choice, borrow "Curious George" by H. A Rey, "Monkeys and Apes" by Kathryn Wentzel Lumbey, or "A Monkey's Tale" by Nathan Kravetz.

If the child is older, choose one of the special exhibits, like the herpetorium where they exhibit reptiles and amphibians. Again, choose several books from the library before you go.

If you are lucky enough to have the children spend both days of the weekend with you, then read stories about the animals on Saturday, and make the trip to the zoo the next day. If that's not possible, start or end the day with the storytelling, or bring the book to the zoo with you. Bring newspapers, a mat, or folding chairs to sit on, and read the story right in front of the animal's zoo home.

If the child is old enough to read by himself, help him learn to use books to find out more about the animal he is seeing. You might find out some interesting facts about the animals you are planning to see, and prepare yourself with a few good questions about them such as, "What is a pit viper?" and "Which snakes that you are seeing are pit vipers?" or "Do all frogs live in water?"

If you call ahead to the zoo, you can find out the feeding schedule. Plan to be at the animal abode 10-15 minutes before the feeding keeper arrives. You may want to watch the keepers clean cages, as well. The zoo office will usually let you know if anything special is planned with your favorite animal on the day you plan to come. Some animals get groomed, manicured, medicated, and so forth on special schedules.

It is very interesting to visit the zoo when it is not crowded. If you plan a trip during the winter there will be fewer visitors and you'll enjoy seeing the animals who are more active in colder climates.

Some zoos allow you to bring a gift of food for the animals to be given to the feeding keeper. If you have a fruit tree, or have gone apple-picking and gathered too much fruit, or if you have a quantity of bread, muffins and buns, the zoo may accept these food gifts. Again, call the zoo before bringing anything.

When you get home from the zoo trip, take the cookie dough out of the refrigerator and follow the directions for making cookies. Use the animal cookie cutters or cardboard shapes to help you make a cookie zoo. Use raisins or currants for eyes. Enjoy eating the cookies after they have been cooled.

The next time you plan a trip to the zoo, visit a different animal and learn about that one ahead of time.

3
FERRY TRIP

Most ferryboats can carry cars, so you may want to drive your car on board. Prepare a picnic lunch to eat on board, or when you land. Add extra bread or crusts to feed seagulls.

Find out ahead of time about the port that the ferry leaves from. You can call or write the ferry company or harbor master and find out what kinds of boats the children will probably see, what other landmarks might be visible, and information about the landing port. Find out how long the trip takes and prepare to keep the children occupied while on board.

Bring sweaters because even on a hot day, it gets breezy on the water. If the weather is cold, bundle up in hats, scarves and mittens, in addition to warm coats. Note where the bathrooms are. Children need to use the restroom immediately after getting cold, and frequently thereafter.

Choose several books from the library about boats that might be observed on your trip. Enjoy some childhood favorites like "Tuggy the Tug-boat" by Jean Horton Berg, "Big City Port" by Betty Maestro, or "Harbor" by Donald Crews.

Take photographs. If you drive your car on the boat, make sure to get a picture of it on board. The children will enjoy the memory of the day the car took a trip!

4
PHOTOGRAPHY

Taking Photographs Photography, like stamp collecting, is a hobby that can stay with you for life. Your child can start this hobby by taking simple photographs and mounting them in an album. He can also learn skills in picture-taking, developing film, and printing pictures. If you both share this hobby, the two of you can attend photo club meetings, shows, seminars, and submit photographs to shows and contests together.

Eastman Kodak(TM) publishes a book called "The Joy of Photography" and a large number of individual bulletin size manuals, all of which are excellent for a teen or adult. In addition, there are many books in the library on photography, in both the adult and the children's sections, some of which are listed below:

- "Complete Photography Course" by John Hedgecoe
- "Time-Life Library of Photography"
- "Photography Basics" by Vince Owens-Knudsen
- "Instant Photography" by Lon Jacobs, Jr.

Modern cameras, even the most complex, are simple to use. The camera often uses micro-chips to figure lens openings and focus. Introduce children to picture-taking before introducing camera techniques. Allow them the freedom of using the film as they see fit. Don't restrict the number of pictures that they may take of one subject. If you are budget-conscious, tell the children ahead of time how many pictures they can take. It is best to develop a roll of film as soon after you take the pictures as possible. Don't be over-generous in the number of rolls you allow them to use if you can't develop them all right away.

After a child has had the opportunity to take several rolls of pictures, find out from him which photographs please him the most. Help him discover why those pictures are especially pleasing to him, and what he did to achieve that result. Help him develop a critical eye without destroying his creativity.

After the child has developed some confidence in picture-taking, you can start introducing some knowledge of what the camera can do and some simple techniques.

Introduce the photographic rule of thirds, that helps you position a subject in your picture in the most visually-pleasing location. Think of the total area of your photograph as being seen through a tick-tack-toe screen, and then place the main subject at one of the crossing points.

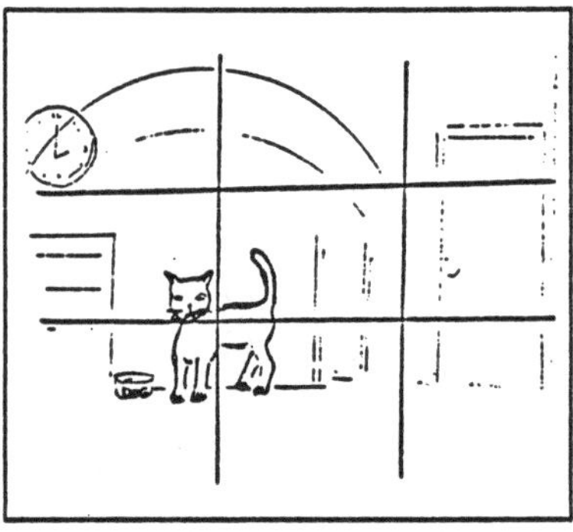

Another way to take an exciting picture is to fill the entire viewing area with the subject.

Help your children learn to choose the correct distance for taking a picture. One good way to teach your child this skill is to take several experimental pictures of the same subject. Pose a person in good light with a tree, large rock, or brick well directly behind them. Measure the distance from where the subject will be. Mark the ground with chalk or a small rock at 6', 10', 25', and 40'. Take a photograph and then move to the next mark and take the next photo. The result will be a group of very similar pictures ranging from long distance to close-up.

There are many "tricks" to taking good photographs, but most are easily learned. An older child might enjoy some of the tricks for taking pictures of motion. To make a sharp, clear photograph of a moving object, move the camera along the same plane as the action (panning). To show that something is moving, brace or mount the camera on a tripod and keep the camera still while the activity crosses in front of the lens. The resulting picture will show streaks of movement.

To brace a camera when you don't have a tripod, you can rest your elbows on a wall or you can lean your back against a wall or another person's back, while holding the camera firmly. A parked car or other still object can also be used to help you brace your camera.

There are other fun projects that you can do to learn more about the camera and picture-taking. Take 3-5 pictures of the same subject from different sides. Try taking them from different angles, too. Position yourself above, below, or at an angle from the subject. Children frequently like to turn the camera at an angle while taking pictures, but they will probably end up taking most of them on the vertical or horizontal after learning how difficult it is to look at them in an album.

If you have a whole day to spend together, try taking the same picture early in the morning, mid-morning, high noon, mid-afternoon, early evening, and at night. Use the same subject, posed the same way and keep notes on the time and exposure number. When the pictures are printed, lay them out in the correct order and discover together the differences in shadow length, as well as shadow direction.

Children as young as nine or ten can learn about developing film and making black and white prints. Join a photography group at a neighborhood center together. If the children seem very interested, you can start to develop black and white film at home, easily and inexpensively.

Printing Photographs Printing B/W pictures is a bit more expensive and takes up more room but it can be done in many bathrooms. If you already have an enlarger-printer, introduce the children to printing by making photograms or object pictures.

Gather an assortment of small flat objects with interesting shapes. Use everyday, simple things like keys, screws, washers, small tools, measuring spoons, spiral springs from ball point pens, coins, paper clips, fasteners, and so on.

Prepare your "dark room" for printing by setting up all your chemical trays. In the darkened room, prepare a sheet of photography print paper on the base of the printer, or use a desk lamp as the light source. Lay the assortment of small objects on the paper. Turn the printer or lamp light on for a few seconds. Turn it off, and remove the objects. Develop the print. You can make several different prints, rearranging the items each time. It is also possible once the children see the result, to plan the specific placement of objects to create a design. Try using natural objects like leaves, dried grasses, rocks, ferns, flowers, and even bug-chewed leaves instead of manufactured items. Try making photograms using paper cut-outs, or any of the above combined with each other.

Frame the prints and hang them in the children's room or hallway. You can use the photograms or your favorite photographs for next year's holiday greeting cards. Most photo stores can give you information on making cards, and even on making posters from your photographs.

5
A TRIP TO THE CIRCUS

A trip to the circus is, by definition, an entertaining day, but it can often become unduly expensive and exhausting. Make your trip the most fun by planning to arrive at the circus grounds or arena at least a half hour before starting time so that you can park and find your seats easily. Tie a strip of colored ribbon, cloth, or a balloon to your antenna so that you can find your car quickly after the circus is over.

Decide ahead of time, and let the children know, how much money each child can spend. There are so many vendors walking up and down the aisles, that the children will be overwhelmed. Help them think about the purchases they can make before they go to the circus. Most circus sales are for food, candy, drinks, circus-lights, small toys, coloring books, and sometimes small reptiles like chameleons.

It's a good idea to have lunch and drinks, and to use the bathroom at home before you leave. This cuts down on the need for food and drinks at the circus. If your youngsters need frequent trips to the bathroom, take them before going to your seats. If you have a problem taking a little girl to the bathroom, plan this trip to the circus (and other large public places) with other couples or single parents. Share the responsibility for making the bathroom trips and for caring for the children who remain in their seats. If the weather is cold, make sure that, when you take your seats, the children remove all their outer clothing before they sit down.

The most exhausting part of the circus is watching what is happening in all the rings. Observe your children. If they appear to get frustrated trying to watch it all, direct their interest to one area. Show them how to watch just one ring for a while, or look at just one acrobatic act. The acts last long enough to watch each one, alone, for a period of time.

During the intermission break, stand up at your seats and do a few simple exercises to stretch and unkink. At intermission, make sure that their outer clothing is still arranged neatly on their chairs so that they will be comfortable for the last half of the show. Now is a good time to buy the special item that you planned with them.

When you get home in the evening, you might want to make a clown-face fruit salad as described in the cooking chapter. Give the children time to talk about their day. Talking will help them relax enough to fall asleep.

6
APPLE PICKING

Going apple picking (or any other kind of orchard picking) is a fun trip for an urban or suburban child. Most cities are within driving distance of the country, and a day planned in the country can be very special. Plan a picnic lunch, including drinks. Add a few damp wash cloths (in plastic bags) to the picnic package, for washing up after lunch.

Most farms that allow picking, charge a per-car entrance fee, and/or a per-basket of picked fruit or exit fee, but are still fairly economical. Don't over pick. You can only eat so many of one kind of any fruit before it either starts to rot or you get tired of it.

Walk among the trees with your children. Visit with other people picking or picnicking. If the orchard has more than one type of apple, examine the varieties with the children and show them the differences.

Apple-picking is another of the trips that is fun to share with other families, so plan it as a large group activity.

Return to the same place next spring when the orchard is in blossom and then in the summer when the fruit is developing to show the children what the apples look like in their various stages. Take photographs throughout the year. Take a trip past the orchard in the winter, on the way to a ski trip.

7
VISIT AN ART MUSEUM

It is possible to walk into a museum and just wander from room to room. Most museums are designed to exhibit different styles and periods of art, and include art objects, statues, paintings, and frequently furniture and costumes.

You can enjoy an unrushed stroll or you can plan to spend time at a special exhibit. There is always a good amount of publicity about new exhibits in both the news and entertainment sections of the newspaper. Don't take children to a new exhibition during the first few days or the first couple of weekends. There are usually crowds when the show is new. Make your visit at a time when the children won't get pushed aside by adults.

Check in your library for material on the artist or style of special exhibits so that you and the children can be informed about them beforehand. If you are hoping to develop an awareness of the fine arts in your children, make the museum a special place. Don't let them get tired or bored.

Check out some children's books about art, and others about drawing. Give them a chance to try some art work on their own prior to seeing what famous artists have done. A talented child might demonstrate a knowledge of art that surprises you.

The "Young People's Story of Fine Art" by V.M. Hillyer and E.G. Huey and "The History of Art" by Norbet Lynton are two suggestions for books that can introduce your child to the art world and then continue to inform them as they get more involved.

You might want to buy some prints of famous pictures that are hanging in the museum for your home. Most museums have a shop that sells prints, calendars, and other art items. Many museum shops also carry post cards, which are inexpensive and easy to handle. After you buy a print, search for the painting in the museum so that the children can see the original. Point out the similarities and differences between the print and the original. You might find a print that would look good in the child's room. Owning a good copy helps develop an awareness of fine art.

8
COUNTY OR STATE FAIRS

Plan to attend the Fair on a day which has a scheduled activity that is special for your child. If your youngsters belong to a club like FFA, 4-H, or the Scouts, they may find it especially exciting to attend the Fair when one of those groups is putting on a special performance or show. If your child has a garden, a pet, a farm animal, a special hobby, or collection, be sure to see the exhibits for that particular interest.

There is usually enough advance time before the Fair arrives to plan what you will do and see. Use that time to also rehearse safety plans. Take instant pictures of the children, wearing the clothes they will wear on Fair day. Keep the pictures with you in case the children get lost. As soon as you get to the fair grounds, point out the place where you will all meet in case anyone gets separated from the group. Point out what the security police look like so that the children will recognize them as policemen, despite their unfamiliar uniforms.

Take along a wet wash cloth in a plastic bag. Not only can it be used for cleaning, but it can also be used for cooling a hot child. If it's very hot or sunny, wear caps. Carry a thermos or container of cold water for drinking.

If you plan to go on any of the rides in the amusement park, be sure they are safe for small children and are not frightening. Eat after going on the rides, not before. Take lots of pictures.

9
PLANETARIUM

Plan to make your visit to a planetarium at a time when they have scheduled a children's show. Many planetariums have different shows or methods of presenting their shows for adult audiences.

Most children are so taken by the dramatic "sky" projected on the ceiling of the planetarium that they have difficulty, at first, following the lecturer's dialogue. Prepare them for the event by telling them what to expect. If possible, take them to the country prior to the trip to the planetarium. Point out how much clearer the evening and night sky is, in a place where the city lights don't reflect against the sky. You might point out how the reflection of lights against city buildings even shows up on T.V. weather maps as "clutter."

Explain the difference between astronomy and astrology. Help the children realize that the names of star groupings have been used by astrologers as birth signs to describe the positions of the sun and the moon at the time of one's birth, but that this is the only similarity between the studies.

If the children have watched science-fantasy or fiction films or T.V. programs like Star Trek, they may already be familiar with star names like Antares or planet names like Saturn or Pluto, or the names of systems like the Milky Way or Andromeda galaxies. They may also have heard of comets, meteorites, and shooting stars. The words will not all be new and strange. As a matter of fact, listen to what they have to say after a planetarium trip; you may be surprised by how well informed they are.

10
FLY KITES

If you plan on flying kites with very young children, purchase the largest, brightest, most colorful, and least breakable kite available. Then buy a second as a spare.

Save the cardboard roller tube from toilet tissue. Buy several balls of kite string, then tie the string around the roller, and scotch tape the short loose end to the cardboard tube. Wind the entire ball of string on the roller tube. Knot the end of the second ball of string to the first, and keep on winding it. Keep the extra ball of string for the extra kite.

Push a large dowel, or a piece of closet hanger rod, or broom stick (about 12" long), through the cardboard roller to use as a handle. A child can hold both sides of the handle while avoiding cuts or string burns from the rapidly spinning string.

An older child might like to make his own kite after using a commercial one successfully. He might also become interested in some of the more involved Japanese kites or commercially-made kites used for weather analysis.

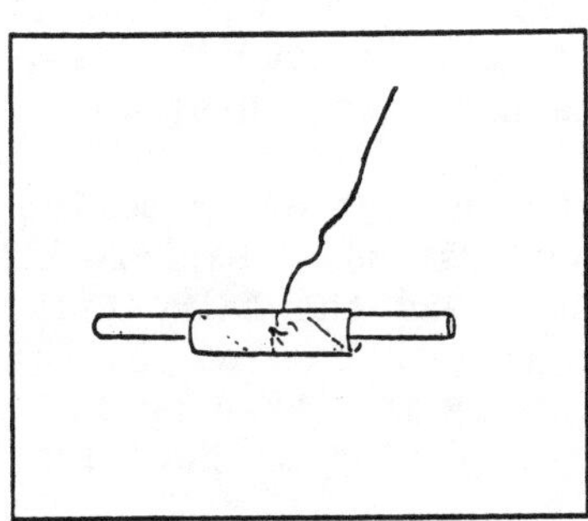

Among the interesting kite books to be found in the library, are the following:

- "A Kite Over Tenth Avenue" by Joan M. Lexar
- "Kites to Make and Fly" by Jack Newnham
- "The Berenstain Bears Go Fly a Kite" by Stan Berenstain
- "Kites" by Tsutomu Hiroi

For those who become very interested in kite-flying, there are several kite-flying contests and competitions held annually all over the country in which it might be fun to participate.

11
BALLET

All children should have the opportunity of an introduction to the performing arts, but the opportunity should be on a level that the child enjoys. A wonderful introduction to the ballet can take place if the child sees a ballet whose story is familiar. Fairy tales like "The Doll Maker," which is danced as "Coppelia" and the story of "Cinderella," have been choreographed as ballets. Read and discuss the story with your child so that he will have an idea, ahead of time, about what is happening on stage.

Explain the concept of symbolism to a child old enough to understand. Explore the differences between reality and the fairy-tale aspects of the story being danced in the ballet. Talk about staging and costumes. Prepare the child for stage effects that might be frightening, like fire or smoke.

Introduce the child to other kinds of choreographed dance, such as the folk dancing style done in the ballet "Rodeo." See a modern ballet. If the child is old enough to enjoy them, see the ballets presented by the dance companies of other countries.

Treat an older child to the gala atmosphere of an evening performance. Treat the occasion as a dress-up affair and arrive early enough to people-watch.

Be aware that many children become involved on a very personal level with what is going onstage. They tend to become so absorbed that they "become" the character. They also respond to happy or unhappy endings, becoming very gay or sad. This is a healthy way for children to "feel" strong emotions in a safe environment.

12
SAIL TOY BOATS

You can sail toy boats in a tub, pool, stream, pond, or lake. Some parks even have special boat-sailing ponds.

Start with a small paper, cardboard, or plastic boat. Allow it to bob and float in the water. Tie a long thread or string on the boat so that it can easily be retrieved. Make the string light enough so that it doesn't weigh the boat down and cause it to sink. If the child is interested, you may want to investigate making models that can be sailed. Start with a very simple model and as the child's interest grows, so can the complexity and cost of the model.

Radio-controlled models appeal to older children and adults. They are quite expensive but great fun.

If you use nylon thread or fishing-line to control the boat, make sure to collect it before you leave the park. Many water birds get badly hurt or killed when they get caught in the unbreakable line.

13
AQUARIUM

When you visit your city or town's aquarium, expect to see fish of all types; crustaceans, such as lobsters and shrimp; and small animals, such as starfish and anemones. You may also see squid and octopus. Some aquariums also display mammals that live near the sea such as seals and otters, and those that actually live in the sea, such as dolphins.

All marine animals are displayed in tanks, some as tall as a two- or three-storied building. Prepare the children for the building by explaining that at first it may seem dark and have strange colored light in the interior, but that they will acclimate quickly.

Explain beforehand that they may see all kinds of animals living at different levels of the tanks. Animals such as starfish are usually found on the bottom of the tank, just as they are in the ocean. Some types of starfish or sea urchins might cling to rocks on the side of a tank, but generally they stay still and don't swim around.

Point out how the fish use their fins and tails as aids to their swimming. Show them how a school of fish follows their leader and that they all seem to change direction (and leader) simultaneously. See if you can point out a fish disguised to blend in to its background. Most fish are fast; don't expect a small child to see everything the first time that you point it out. Give them several chances to see what you are describing, and then let them try for themselves.

Point out how the water temperature is maintained. Show the children where the clean water comes into the tank if the mechanics for maintenance are visible.

A trip to the aquarium can be very relaxing if you are prepared ahead of time with answers. The water in the tanks seems to relax both parents and children alike.

If you have been thinking that you might like a pet in your new home, this might be a good time to decide on a small home aquarium.

Visit an aquarium shop or pet store. Show the children all of the things that you will need for a home aquarium. Point out that, just like the large aquarium, you, too, will need a thermostat, heater, light,and a filtration system for your little tank.

The most economical home aquarium system is one for fresh-water fish. Salt water aquariums need more precise care and the fish are more expensive. Some aquarium fish breed easily, and breeding and raising fish might be the beginning of an interesting hobby for you and the children to share.

14
TRAIN MUSEUM

Most children start learning all about the transportation industry in the lower grades of school. Trains are important in telling the history of this country, and older children might be interested in reading about trains and how they opened the country for settlers. Some books are on trains include:

- "The Train Book" by John Johnson
- "Train Coming" by Betty Ren Wright
- "Train Talk" by Roger B. Yepsen
- "Trains" by Ray Broekel.

If you still have any of your own toy electric trains, take them out of storage. Let the children examine them and discover that a toy train collection may contain many kinds of trains and train cars, and that these are a sampling of the real world. Talk about the different kinds of cars and what they were used for. Point out the different train names on the boxcars. Once they have discovered how much there is to find out about trains, visit a train museum.

Most train museums have examples of different kinds of engines, including coal-driven, diesel, and electric engines. The children will also be able to see the changes that have been made in the construction of produce, cattle and refrigerator cars. They can learn about some of the larger train lines and the initials, names, and logos associated with them.

Some train museums have films, talks, and demonstrations while others have train rides available on antique or narrow tracks. Write ahead or call for a brochure to find out if the train museum has any special events planned in the near future.

15
HISTORICAL WALKING TOUR

You can plan an historical tour for your own city or town, or you can visit a nearby area.

Do a little research before making your trip. Plan the trip around people, places, or events. There is usually a historical society in most areas that can supply you with information, as can many motor clubs. Look for special markers on roads and highways. Before your trip, visit the library. Borrow books with stories about the places to which you are going. If there is a play, movie, video, or television program about the place you plan to visit, be sure to see it.

Once you have arrived, take photographs so that you can make your own book about the visit. If there is a series of places to see, start at the one with the earliest historical importance so that you can build on the experience. Don't try to do all of the tours in one day.

Dress appropriately for the weather. Plan a picnic lunch or eat in a restaurant close to the historical site. Don't get over tired. Make this a relaxing day.

16
CHILDREN'S THEATER

Plays for children are presented by professional and amateur theater groups, libraries, colleges, churches, and synagogues. Read the promotional material about the play. Most play advertisements state which age they appeal to.

The humor in children's theater is broader than in adult theater. There are lots of pratfalls and predictable happenings. Children's senses of humor are different at different ages, and change frequently. Expect lots of giggling, and surprised expressions. Even if the outcome of a story seems predictable and obvious, children see it as new and unexpected.

Once a child has seen a play, don't be surprised if he wants to see it again. A child often finds it especially enjoyable to see the story again when he already knows the ending.

If your budget can handle it, get a pictorial program for the play. Your children may be able to recall a little about what they have seen from the regular program, but the photographs in the more expensive program will help remind them of what they have seen.

17
TRIP TO AN AIRPORT

Take this opportunity to show the children what you do when you go on a business trip. Plan your trip to the airport as though you were actually planning to go somewhere. If you are planning a business trip in the near future, purchase your tickets when you are at the airport with the children. Park your car in the parking lot. Tie a ribbon to the antenna, so that it will be easier to find.

Take the airport bus from the parking area to the terminal. Show the children where the Skycaps pick up luggage outside the terminal and how they tag it for the correct flight. Move into the terminal and show the children the announcement boards or video terminals that show the names, times, and gates for the day's flights. Point out the ticket desks for the different airlines. Make your ticket purchase.

Go to the gate area of the terminal. Pass through the inspection area. Prepare the children for this area. If Security doesn't mind, you may be allowed to stand behind the inspector who is viewing hand luggage. Show the children what the security agent sees in the luggage and handbags.

Spend some time at the gate, itself. Watch the planes from the window. Point out planes taxiing to the runway, as well as planes taking off or landing. If it is visible, point out the FAA tower.

People watch. It's fun to make up stories about the people coming into the airport, or families meeting someone special. Point out different styles of dress and different nationalities. Point out the gate from which you normally leave on business trips as well as the ones to which you return. Show the children where the arriving passengers get their luggage.

See if it is possible to show the children how valises are loaded, how the plane is fueled, and how food is brought to the plane.

If your airport has commercial hangars, you may be able to drive nearer to them.

Sometime in the future, try to visit a small airport where the children can get closer to the airplanes and watch the activity.

18
CANDY OR ICE CREAM FACTORY

When planning a visit to a candy factory, or any other factory tour that deals with food, feed the children first.

Most tours end with a free sample of the product they are making. They also have a shop filled with the product at the end of the tour. A comfortably full child can usually be satisfied with the sample. This is another place where it will be a good idea to carry a damp wash cloth in a plastic bag.

Although most tour guides welcome questions, teach the children to ask them politely, and without interrupting. Explain that not everyone has been taught good manners, and that they may see other children or adults act unmannerly. Explain that poor behavior is still not right even if others don't know better. Make sure that the children can see what is being displayed.

The next time that you purchase the product in the market, remind the children of the time they saw it being made.

19
BIKE RIDING

When you plan a bike trip, check out all the safety measures first. Be sure that the bikes are in good condition with all bolts and screws properly tightened, and all chains moving smoothly and lubricated. Be sure that the handlebars and seats are in comfortable positions and that all bikes have reflectors. Wear bike helmets, if possible.

Choose a bike path that is safe from traffic and pedestrians. Carry a first-aid kit including sun screen and insect repellent. Bring along a water-bottle.

Do not plan a trip that is too long. Gauge the total distance that all of you can enjoy riding without getting too tired, and don't exceed that amount. Consider the places where you have to go up hills and down hills when you do your planning. Plan the length of a trip based on the abilities of the weakest member of the group.

Bike trips can be planned with children of different ages. Allow the older children to ride ahead. Plan an activity for them to do when they arrive at the destination. Have them set up a rest or refreshment area or read until you and the youngest children arrive at the pre-planned location.

20
STREET FAIR

Street fairs usually emphasize games-of-chance, food, and family fun. Most are fund-raising efforts by churches or community centers. Many street fairs are ethnic.

Plan your excursion at a meal-time and introduce the children to new kinds of food. Bring along some simple foods, like peeled carrots and crackers, for the child too young or too hesitant to try something new.

Sometimes artists display their paintings at these fairs. You might find an attractive piece of work for your home. It may even be possible to watch the artists and crafts people at work. Very often mimes, clowns, or puppeteers put on shows at such street fairs.

Make sure the children use the bathroom before leaving home. Check to see if portable bathrooms have been set up for the public's use. Don't let any child enter a public bathroom alone. Check the portable toilet to make sure it is empty and clean enough to use before allowing your child to use it. It might be a good idea to carry tissues, to be used as toilet paper.

If it is possible, make a second visit to the fair at night when all the booths are lit up and the streets sparkle with displays and lights.

21
PLANT A FLOWER BOX OR GARDEN

Whether you plant a garden, a pot, or a flower-box with young child, choose a very fast germinating seed like a bean or radish.

Plant seeds that reward the child with something to see, smell, or taste. Plant two pots or divide a flower box so that you can plant flowers and vegetables. There are some tomato plants, called patio tomatoes, that will grow in a pot. Fast flowering seeds that are very reliable are marigold, zinnia, and, as mentioned, radish.

Label the pots including the name of the plant, the date you planted it, and the number of days to germination and flower (or fruit).

Give your plants the proper amounts of light and water as described on their packaging. Don't allow a plant that you and your child have grown together to die of neglect. Develop a watering, weeding, and feeding schedule.

Visit a garden nursery and point out the different ways plants grow, and the many ways they start out. Show the children examples of seed sizes, bulbs, tubers, cuttings, and transplants. When your own flowers are mature, you can inspect the ripe flower heads to discover where the new seeds come from. Save some seeds in an envelope for planing another time.

If you discover worms and bugs when you dig in the dirt, you can discuss the function of earthworms and other "good" bugs. When your garden yields a fair-sized crop, share the harvest. Plan with the children to give away some of the vegetables and choose the lucky recipients together.

22 FISHING

Keep fishing simple and hopefully rewardable. Take the children fishing at a location where it is possible to really catch something. Explain beforehand that sometimes you can catch fish and sometimes you can't, and that sometimes one person can catch several, while the very next person catches none. Don't allow them to develop the expectation that catching a fish is guaranteed.

Fishing can be a very relaxing sport but it can also be dangerous. Make sure that all safety rules are followed. Not only are rocks, shores, and piers slippery in fishing areas, but other fishermen can cause accidents. Warn the children about walking behind fishermen who are casting their lines. Be prepared with the name and location of the closest emergency room handling fish-hook injuries.

Prepare the bait (live and manufactured) before the trip. Explain the use of each, and the care and handling of the bait. Older children may enjoy learning about fly-tieing and would be interested in books like "Freshwater Fish and Fishing" by Jim Arnowsky or "Fishing" by Paul G. Neimark.

You might also like to read the Boy Scouts of America Merit Badge book on fishing. There are merit badge books filled with information on many topics and they are excellent resources.

Teach respect for other fishermen. Some fishermen insist on silence, while others don't mind quiet conversation. Some fishermen like to talk about their catches. If they don't mind, you may be able to let the children look in their buckets and examine their catches.

Be patient, but don't expect patience. Be prepared with other activities.

23
TREASURE HUNT

There are several different kinds of treasure hunts that are fun to plan with children.

Metal Detector Treasure Hunt The first treasure hunt requires a metal detector and a good searching place. If you own a metal searching device, plan a day at the beach or the park. The best time of the year is the late fall, winter, or early spring when the beach or park is not crowded, and before it becomes too hot. Wear a hat or cap, and wear clothes with a collar that can be turned up to protect the back of your neck from wind or sun. Carry a cloth sack for your treasures.

Mystery Treasure Map - Treasure Hunt Another kind of treasure hunt requires that you visit a "treasure" site before the children do. Bring a tape measure with you for noting the distance between objects. Draw a map, or write instructions that give directions to find the treasure. If the search is to be in an area that is private, you can hide a small prize.

Clues for the hunt might include instructions like these:

> "Start at the big oak in the corner of the yard. Take 6 steps toward the shed, and turn right. ..."

Measure off the distances with the tape measure and then translate the figure into steps, using the length of the child's normal step.

If the instructions for the treasure hunt are for an area that is unfamiliar to the children, and commonly used by others, you will have to leave a note or message at the final destination instead of the prize. Bring transparent tape or thumb tacks for hanging the message. The reward or prize can be special plans for another day, a small gift, or an ice cream sundae.

<u>The Search - Treasure Hunt</u> A third kind of treasure hunt can be part of a day at the beach, the park, the zoo, and so on. Make a list ahead of time of things the children should be able to find. Make some of the items on the list easy to find and others more difficult. If two or more children are participating, arrange the lists in different order, so that they don't just follow each other around.

You might give hints like the following for a zoo trip:

- Find an animal that has stripes, and is not a member of the cat family.
- Write down it's name. How many are there in the cage?

Make the list simple for very young children, more complex and meaningful for the older children.

At the beach or park, the children can collect a variety of things listed in the instructions like shells, pebbles, leaves of specific shapes, twigs, bugs, and so on.

24
MAKE A BIRTHDAY PARTY

Very often birthdays come at a time when you can't be with the child, or the child's mother is having a party and you are not invited. Make your own birthday party. Invite your parents and the new friends that the children have made in your neighborhood. If that is not possible, make a private party for just you and your kids.

Many bakeries will decorate a regular cake for a very small fee or no fee at all, or you can buy an ice-cream cake or decorate cupcakes instead of a large cake. Put one candle into each cupcake.

You don't have to go to the expense of party plates and cups. Use regular paper plates, but use birthday napkins. (Napkins can be opened up to serve as placemats as well as napkins.) Use the birthday present as the centerpiece--it deserves being displayed.

By making your own special celebrations, you don't miss out on special events.

25
SET UP ELECTRIC TRAINS

It might be fun to set up toy trains that will be waiting for the children on their visits to your home. Postage-stamp or "N" gauge trains are very small although quite accurate. They may be too small for a little child to handle, but a youngster seven or eight years old should be able to manipulate them.

Begin with a starter set. A set usually contains 25 feet of track, an engine, and 3 to 5 cars. Add to the track over a period of time. Purchase a building or a building kit. It is possible to buy everything in postage-stamp or "N" guage that can be bought in larger sizes, but the miniatures can be stored in very little space.

When you have decided on a layout that you all like, make it permanent. Attach the tracks to a half or third-sheet of plywood. Make the base a size that can fit into a closet. You can also attach the tracks to the underside of a bridge-table, which can then easily be flipped upside-down to be used for the track layout (yet get ordinary use as a table). It can be folded flat and stored.

Once you have decided where you will have your train layout, you can paint on roads, streets, and town markings. After you arrange the permanent layout, you can add glued-on grass and shrubs. (They won't get in the way during storage.) Set up trees, houses, stations, tunnels, buildings, and the trains when you take the board out of its hiding place.

You can keep adding to the set-up and it is always fun to go to the hobby shop or the train store to buy a new kit or train.

26
BOTANICAL GARDENS

You will find that a trip to the botanical gardens will be different at different times of the year. Most botanical gardens have rose gardens, bulb or spring gardens, fall chrysanthemum or aster displays, and Christmas evergreen and poinsettia displays.

Your children may get bored just walking and looking, so plan to see special things with them. Children are often fascinated by "the biggest," "the tallest," "the oldest," "the wettest or the driest," and so on.

Many greenhouse displays are built to resemble the geographical areas that the plants come from, and therefore, feel like a jungle, desert, rain-forest, or swamp. Some include birds, small animals, or reptiles.

Many botanical gardens have plants for sale. If you don't have the time to care for a large plant, you may want to purchase a cactus. There are so many different kinds of cacti and succulents that it is interesting to make a choice.

27
SNOW SKIING

Skiing is a sport that goes against every person's instinctive sensibilities. You must go out into the coldest weather, attach two immense sticks to your feet, push yourself down a hill with two other sticks, hurtle yourself into space, and learn to fall down. Yet, skiing is the greatest fun.

When you take young children skiing, expect them to be interested in the snow, not the sport. They don't get the endurance, patience, or musculature to actually ski until they are at least eight to twelve years-old. But, don't hesitate to take them to beginning slopes or flat areas where they can learn to walk in their heavy ski boots and skis. Allow them to play in the snow while wearing their skiing equipment. Keep them from playing at the base of the hill, where they might get hurt by an out-of-control skier or a runaway ski.

The best way to keep warm when skiing is to layer clothes. A child can wear leotards, and over the leotards he or she can wear long john underwear and thin socks. Over that, goes heavy work socks, a turtleneck shirt, ski-pants, or lined jeans. If it is very cold, add a long-sleeved wool sweater. A ski jacket or lift coat goes over everything. Thin gloves are covered with leather mittens. Your child's wool hat should cover his ears and his eyes should be protected with goggles.

Children's clothes tend to separate at the waist, so suspenders might be a good idea. Remember that after all these clothes are on, your child will have to go to the bathroom.

Do some warm-up exercises together before you start to ski, including some stretching and loosening warm-ups. Take frequent breaks so that the children don't get overly tired. Watch for signs of frostbite.

If you are a very confident skier, you can take your child up the hill on the lift, and assist him in coming down. Don't make these first trips on a steep hill until you are both confident. Never allow small children to go on a lift, T- or J-Bar, or use a rope-tow without an adult caring for them.

Older children and teenagers can quickly out ski their parents. As soon as a child's body matures enough for him to develop the stomach, back, and thigh muscles used in skiing, they learn quickly, and because they started when they were young, they rapidly become agile in the sport.

Expect the children to fall asleep in the car on the way home. All the cold fresh air seems to knock them out.

28
GO TO A MAGIC SHOW

Most children have had the opportunity to see magic tricks performed on T.V. and are familiar with the names of many magicians. They have a level of sophistication that makes magicians work extra hard to design their effects.

When you go to a "live" magic show, try to purchase your seats at front center. (Depending on its popularity, it may be necessary to purchase those tickets the very moment that you hear any publicity for the show.) Before the show, keep any ideas you have on how a performance is done to yourself. Let the magic be the message.

After the show, if the children are interested, you can talk about how the tricks were done. You might even like to visit a magic store to watch amateurs and professionals try out new tricks, or buy some tricks yourselves.

29
ATTEND A PRO FOOTBALL GAME

A professional football game is football, cheerleaders, atmosphere, people, weather, excitement, color, and when the ball isn't being moved, dull. Keep your neighbors happy; do your explaining during he lulls in the activity.

If you live in a cold climate, dress warmly for the game. Layer your clothes like you would for skiing. Bring a blanket to sit on because most bleacher seats are cold. Bring a thermos or two of hot cocoa and a small towel for spills. Take along sandwiches and a dessert snack like cookies or doughnuts. Spot the bathrooms. Cold children need to relieve themselves frequently.

You might think about taking a small portable radio to help clarify the decisions being made by the referees. Decide beforehand whether the children can purchase banners, flags, or treats. Determine the amount that can be spent by each child.

After the game, in the warmth of your living room, watch the sports news for highlights of the game.

30
HOT AIR BALLOON SHOW

Start the day by strolling around the field while the balloonists unload their trucks and vans. Notice the colors on the balloons. Many of the trucks and chase cars are painted the same colors, or bear flags in the same colors as the balloon.

Watch the teams spread the balloons out on the grass. They set up the baskets and check the gas jets that are used for heating the air. Some teams will accept your help setting up their balloons.

Make sure that you bring a camera. With all the excitement and all the color, almost every photograph you take is perfect. You can watch the teams inflate the balloons with a powered fan until it is upright enough to heat the air. Then they turn on the gas-powered flames and warm the inside of the balloon until it stands erect. The balloon gets attached to the basket and becomes ready for passengers.

There are several different kinds of races and contests held at balloon shows. You might want to read about them or about balloon stories. An old favorite, which has been made into a film, is "Around the World in 80 Days."

Many balloonists allow children to take tethered rides. They take children into the balloon basket and then rise 30-50 feet into the air. A tethered ride is a great ending to a hot air balloon show.

31
GLUE AND WOOD SCULPTURE

Collect chunks and pieces of wood scrap from a wood-working shop or cabinet maker. Save pieces up to a foot in length. Include wood turned on a lathe or shaped wood from dowels or closet rods. When you have a good assortment, hand the box of wood and a large bottle of white or tacky glue to your child.

Show the child the technique for gluing wood together and then let him create a free form wood sculpture. Make sure that all work is done on a plastic drop cloth or newspaper. When it is dry, you may want to paint or spray it.

32
GO BOWLING

Like many other sports, a child cannot participate in bowling correctly until the appropriate musculature and strength has developed. However, many bowling alleys have pint-sized balls that the children can throw down the alleys like "10 Pins."

When a child is old enough to hold and release a light weight ball, (don't expect a very young child to know how to release a ball), start watching garage sales for an appropriate weight ball. Have the ball filled in and pre-drilled for your child's span, and then polished to remove nicks and pits. With the correct equipment, your youngster will have the opportunity to become a good bowler.

Although you should get a ball specifically meant for each individual child, you will find that it's a good idea to rent shoes until the child's feet are fully grown.

A child who is old enough to play three full games without tiring can join a weekend team. There are parent/children teams at some alleys. You might want to start one if there are none in your area.

33 GO TO THE PARK

A trip to your own neighborhood park can be a very pleasant way to spend an afternoon. Make this a planned excursion, rather than "just something to do to pass time." If there is a playground in your park, spend some time using the play equipment.

Walk all around the perimeter of the park, and then criss-cross it. Take along old bread or bread crusts to feed to pigeons, or to the ducks in the park pond. You might even take along peanuts to throw to the squirrels.

Look for special trees or flowers. Examine rocks and stones. Collect interesting items for your "scrap box."

A trip to your local park is a pleasant ending to any weekend, and is a perfect trip for the very young child.

34 LATCH HOOK A RUG

Latch-hooking is a handcraft that has become very popular. More than one person can work on a large piece of mesh at one time, and the resulting rug can be used as a wall hanging or a floor covering.

Latch-hooking is the craft of tying loops of wool through a large piece of mesh fabric. Each cross bar in the mesh gets a loop knotted through it. When the picture is complete, the loops form the base of the carpet, and their loose ends stand up, packed closely together to form a shag rug.

Many craft stores, arts and crafts catalogs, and hobby stores sell the materials to make a latch-hook rug. You will need the mesh base through which the loops get knotted, which can be bought by the yard. You will also need packages of cut lengths of wool. Or, instead of buying everything separately, you can buy a kit. A kit provides the mesh (pre-stamped with a design), the correct amount of cut wool, and a latch-hooker. The hooker itself looks like a crochet hook with a hinge.

Hooking takes patience, so it is not appropriate for young children. However, an older child or teen may not only enjoy the craft but the continuity that comes with working on the rug each weekend visit.

35
VISIT A HISTORY MUSEUM

People are fascinated by the history of their world, their country, their neighborhood. Notice all the history books, historical novels, biographies, TV specials, and time-machine stories. They appeal to all ages. Children like to see the relationship between events in the past and their own lives today.

Most local, historical museums emphasize the history of the immediate area. It will be easy to point out locations that are familiar to the children.

Plan to spend most of the day in the museum, and let the children find and spend time at exhibits that are particularly interesting to them.

The children may be studying a particular period of history in school, or they may have seen a television program that excites them. Help them find pertinent exhibits. Don't be surprised if they want to explain them to you.

36
COLLECT SEA SHELLS

If you live near the shore or spend time at the beach, you may consider collecting shells. Buy one of the many soft-covered, pocket-sized reference books that the children can enjoy and use, and take it with you on your shelling trips.

Shells can be collected in a pail, a basket, a plastic bag, or a box of any size.

Start your collection by picking any shell that is not broken. Get a large group of shells. When you get home, carefully wash the shells and allow them to dry. Now check your reference book for the names of the shells and label them. Don't write on the shells--write on a label or piece of paper and tape the label on them. Divide different kinds of shells into different boxes.

The next time that you go collecting shells, try to find samples of shells that you don't already have, or look for better or different shells for the collection. Notice the difference in colors, swirls, shapes, and sizes among the different kinds of shells.

You can display the extra, attractive shells, that you don't want to keep in your special collection. Fill a large, clear glass jar with the shells and close the lid on the jar. To complete the project, glue several shells to the jar lid.

Another attractive display is to fill a shallow basket or bowl with shells. Show these on a coffee table.

As your collection grows, you may want to create permanent display shelves for the more unique or most beautiful.

37
VISIT AN AUTOMOBILE MANUFACTURING PLANT

Planning a trip to an auto plant or any other kind of assembly-line factory includes a great deal of walking. Be prepared to carry a very small child.

Be sure to have lunch and make bathroom trips before starting the tour. Some auto plants have ongoing tours; others insist on appointments for specified tours. Be on time--tour directors don't wait for slowpokes.

Prepare the children for the noise level in the factory. Also remind them of safety rules. Explain that the tour leader will spell out specific safety rules for that tour, but that the children must remember all the family safety rules as well.

Wear comfortable clothes and comfortable shoes. If it is cold weather, take off outer clothes when you get indoors. Keep your sweaters on in the factory; it gets cold.

Find out, ahead of time, if the tour includes film presentations or demonstrations. The children may also be able to receive a memento from the tour. When they get home, help them find a place to display it.

38
FINISH POTTERY GREENWARE

Even if you have no experience making something from pottery, you can learn to do so fairly quickly. Most pottery greenware stores have a large display of all kinds of items to complete, in a wide price range.

Many of these stores have work areas for their customers. Some have classes, too. If you want to work on your pottery at home, keep your sales receipt for the clay form. Kiln fees for baking the object are often based on the price of the clay object when you bought it.

You use simple scraping tools to clean off the mold marks and seams on the clay object. After the clay form is prepared, it gets painted with a glaze. Glazes contain some lead, so watch children very carefully. Make sure they don't put the brush near their mouths. Afterwards, have them wash their hands very thoroughly.

Although the clay is quite fragile when you first get it, it loses that fragility after the first trip to the kiln. Some pottery is complete with one baking while other pieces require additional glazing and firing (baking in the kiln).

Let the children choose one piece each of clay greenware to work on. Help them make a choice of an item small enough to hold easily, finish quickly, and fire inexpensively. If they enjoy working with greenware, they may find this a good way to make gifts for birthdays and holidays.

When the children become knowledgeable about the effects of glazing and the results of firing, you may want to introduce them to the skills displayed by potters who use a wheel or "throw" clay.

39
CARVE A PUMPKIN

Choosing a pumpkin is almost as much fun as carving one. Make the trip and the opportunity to choose the pumpkin an exciting time, whether it is a trip to the country, a produce center, a garden nursery, a farmers' market, or to your own neighborhood market.

Allow the children to make their own choices. Most markets have the pumpkins divided by size and, therefore, cost. Tell each child how much he can spend (if each gets an individual pumpkin), or how much the group can spend. Then, step aside. Bring your camera--you'll delight in the pictures you take of the children making their choices. Take some more pictures when they are carving the pumpkins and add some final ones of the children in costume alongside the lit-up jack-o-lantern.

If you purchase the pumpkins a week or two before Halloween, keep them cold and dry. Don't carve them until the day or the weekend of Halloween.

Wash any dirt off the pumpkin and dry it. Draw

pictures of pumpkin faces on paper first, and then when you are satisfied with a face, draw it on the pumpkin with a washable magic marker or crayon. Make sure that the spacing for eyes or teeth is big enough to allow you to rotate the knife you use for carving.

Cut a circle around the stem. Make it large enough to insert your hand and wrist into the pumpkin. Cut the circle and stem out to use as a lid. Pull out the seeds and the stringy pumpkin material. Toss the seeds into a strainer or colander. Use a large spoon to scrape all the seeds and strings out of the pumpkin, adding the rest of the seeds to those in the colander.

Wash the seeds and lay them on paper toweling to dry. When they are all dry, spread them on a sheet of aluminum foil on a cookie sheet. Lightly sprinkle them with salt. Turn your oven on to 300 degrees and allow it to warm for a few minutes. Put the cookie sheet of seeds into the oven, close the door, and let them bake for 4-6 minutes. When they are cool, they'll be a great snack. Break open the shells and eat the seeds that are inside.

Carve the face of the pumpkin. If any mistakes are made, it doesn't matter. All pumpkins are originals.

Pour a little melted wax into an empty tomato sauce or tuna fish can. Press a candle stub or votive candle into he melted wax. Carve out an indentation in the bottom of the pumpkin into which you can place the can. Light the candle for the children. Put the lid on the pumpkin. Make sure the candle doesn't go out. If it has a hard time burning, cut an air hold for a chimney in the lid. Be careful where you put a pumpkin containing a burning candle. Stay nearby as long as it is lit.

For dessert, have some pumpkin pie or the pumpkin peach salad mentioned in the "Cooking Book" section. As a final touch, read the story of Ichabod Crane, "The Headless Horseman."

40
VISIT A HARBOR

A visit to the harbor should be planned for a time when the most activity is going on. Watch the shipping news section of the newspaper. The newspapers in cities that have harbors list which pleasure ships are docking or leaving.

You may be able to see ships being loaded or unloaded with cargo and luggage. You may also be able to watch the passengers going on board. If the ship is pulling out, you may be able to see the holidaying passengers throw confetti and streamers to their friends on the pier.

Watch the tugs escort the liners from the piers to open water. Watch for ferries, cruise ships, private boats, cargo ships and oil barges. Look for the cranes and derricks used for loading cargo. At some locations, there are sightseeing boats that allow you to see the harbor (and the city) from the water. Watch for firefighting equipment and other special boats.

You may have an aquarium, naval academy, or a branch of the Sea Scouts at your harbor. The areas around some harbors have been spruced up, and now contain shops and boutiques.

41
VISIT A PLAYGROUND

Plan a morning trip to a playground in a different neighborhood and try the equipment there.

Young children enjoy using playground equipment after they have become familiar with it. Most children are not brave enough to try something new without being properly introduced to it. Show them how a different style swing works, how they get on it, and how they get off. Participate in the playground equipment with them. Push swings, or swing in one yourself. You may feel that it's silly for a grown man to be on a swing, but they won't forget the fun. At the most unusual times you may be reminded of the day you went on the swings and seesaw.

42
PLANT FLOWERS FOR AN ELDERLY NEIGHBOR

One of the easiest ways to feel good about yourself is to do something nice for someone else. Share that pleasure with your children by doing something for others, together.

Plant spring flowers or fall bulbs for a neighbor who can't bend easily. Age sometimes makes it difficult to do what is easy for the young. As a result, the elderly have to miss out on things they have always enjoyed.

Offer your services to your neighbor. Although you can offer to buy seeds or bulbs, you may find that the only help needed is for planting. They may want to buy their own bulbs or plants, and they maybe able to weed and water them later. Your job will be to bend down and dig the holes or fill in the holes.

Ask if you can come back to visit when the plants bloom. Let your neighbors know they are under no obligation in return for your service.

43
VISIT A PRAIRIE DOG TOWN

Most prairie dog towns are part of a nature reserve or a larger park. Some of these parks or reserves have interesting exhibits and signs explaining how the prairie dog makes its home.

Although the children will only be able to observe the little rodents above ground, you will be able to use the signs to explain what is going on underground.

Some zoos exhibit prairie dogs in towns that are partially concrete and partially dirt. The concrete barriers keep them from building all over the zoo.

The prairie dogs are fun to watch. They look like excited, tail-less squirrels or oversized chipmunks. They squeak messages to each other and will warn each other back into their holes. These little creatures are inquisitive, and pop right back up to see what the warning was about.

You can spend an interesting hour or two watching these little animals that are rapidly disappearing as prairie dog towns become the location of people cities.

44
POND SKATING

When you plan to go ice-skating outdoors, be sure to bring warm clothes, extra dry socks, and a thermos of hot cocoa.

If you plan to go skating on a pond, be sure that the ice has been tested and declared safe. Make sure that you have emergency equipment with you. A strong rope and several planks should always be at a skating pond for emergency use.

If there has been a recent snow, bring a shovel to clean the ice. For fun, shovel a maze instead of just a path.

Skating is the most fun (and the safest) when you have a large group. Plan to make it a day out for your friends and their children, too.

Make sure that the children have gone to the bathroom before leaving home. Layer their clothing. Several thin layers of clothing are warmer than one heavy layer since the air caught between the layers acts as insulation. Be sure that everyone's skates fit well. Provide ankle supports for weak or unsteady ankles. Do some warm-up exercises before starting to skate. Don't get over tired or chilled. Stop for rest and warm-up breaks, frequently.

45
DOG SHOW

A visit to a dog show is an exciting way to introduce your children to the incredible variation in dog breeds. It is also a way to introduce an awareness of how human beings all vary, but at the same time are all members of the group called people.

A dog show can generally be called a "beauty contest." Unlike the contests that judge attractive women or girls, the dogs are judged against a precise set of standards. To be considered eligible for judging, the animal must first fit into the standards of height, weight, size, coloring, skeletal and muscular structure, and other characteristics.

At shows, the owners or their "handlers" first pose their dogs in a position most appropriate to their breed standards, and then they walk the dogs around in a circle in the show ring. Only dogs of the same breed are judged against each other for the choice of best of the breed. The judging classes are broken down, so that the judging takes place between equals. The classes are divided by sex with the males being called dogs, and females called bitches. Then the classes are divided by age; puppies are judged separately from adults. Immature adults that have not ever won a ribbon, or have won only one or two, have a special division. Adult canines who have significant wins are judged against each other.

The judge examines each dog individually and then has the handler or owner run across the ring at an angle to the judge's vision. The handler follows the judge's instructions to run the dog across the far end of the ring and return to stand in front of the judge. The judge now has the opportunity to see the animal's balance and leg structure as it moves. He is able to determine if the dog meets all the traits defined in the standard for that particular breed and whether the animal looks as good moving as it does posing.

The judge examines all the animals and then chooses the four he deems best in that ring, on that day. He hands each handler of a winner a ribbon: blue for first prize, red for second, yellow for third, and white for fourth. Certain practice shows use other colors for their ribbons.

From among all the dogs and bitches who have won blue ribbons, the judge chooses a best of breed winner and a best of opposite sex to the best of breed winner.

Later on in the day other judges will judge contests among the best of breeds of many different breeds to determine the best example of the breed group (examples are Terrier, Sporting, Working or Toy Group) the animal belongs to. Still later a different judge will determine, from the winners of the six Groups, which animal is the best in the entire show.

A large dog show can take a whole day. Some are held indoors while others are outdoors. Most have vendors who sell snack food or sandwiches and drinks. You might bring a picnic lunch. If you attend an outdoor show, be prepared for a day in the open. Bring sweaters, coats, sun hats, or other appropriate clothing.

There are two special things to see at a dog show besides the breed judging. The first is called the Junior Showmanship classes. In these classes, dogs and bitches already entered in the show in their breed divisions are paraded and shown before another judge. This person judges not the dogs, but the handlers, and all the handlers are children. The children handling these dogs may be very young, but they are not inexperienced. They have worked around dogs most of their lives.

The third area of special judging is obedience judging. The dogs entered in this category have to be pure bred, but do not have to be perfect examples of the breed standard. They do have to be bright and well trained. The obedience judge steps the entire group of dogs in his judging ring through several phases of testing. They must sit, stand, or remain where they are standing, on their owner's commands. The owners are asked to leave the dogs after issuing the command "Stay," and to move out of sight. The animals must remain unmoving, until their owners return, and call them one at a time to "Come." In addition, the dogs and their owners have several other parts of their tests to complete. They gain credits for each stage they complete correctly. Every dog in the ring can finish the test and win. Of course, any and all can also lose. When a dog has won three of these tests, he earns the right to add a degree to his name. The first and easiest to win is the C.D. degree, which stands for Companion Dog, and is worn with as much pride as Champion.

46
HIKING

Hiking should not be confused with merely taking a walk. Hiking is a formal, planned trip to a specific destination. Always prepare yourself and your equipment before you go hiking. If you plan a hike that includes camping out, your preparations will take longer. Never cut down preparation and planning time.

First, you need hiking boots. You should always wear boots that support the foot, the arch, and the ankle. Wear new boots (to get used to them) several times before taking your hike. Wear socks long enough to fold over the tops of the boots. Don't wear short socks, socks that fit poorly, or those that have holes. They can cause sore or rubbed feet and blisters.

The rest of your clothes should be planned according to the weather and temperature. Even in hot weather, plan to carry long pants and a long-sleeved shirt. You may have to cover up to avoid being bitten by mosquitoes and flies. Carry light-weight clothes that can be layered (the process which allows layers of air to become insulation). Bring along a light-weight jacket in case it gets windy or there is a drop in temperature.

Prepare an emergency kit that includes felt or moleskin pads for blisters, a sterile needle, matches, antiseptic, bandages, a collapsible cup, and water-clarifying tablets, as well as any normal medications needed on a full day trip. Add sun-screen lotion and a bug-repellent lotion or spray. Carry a compass and know how to use it.

Make sure that you can recognize poisonous plants such as toadstools, poisonous mushrooms, poison ivy, oak, or sumac, and oleander. Learn how to recognize harmful snakes like rattlers, water moccasins, and copperheads.

Carry a quart of water for drinking, for each person on the hike. Add extra water for cooking.

Take along two small plastic bags, one for garbage and the other for soiled clothes, rock samples, or anything else you might want to collect. Also, carry toilet paper.

If your trip is to be for the entire day, start out with a good breakfast at home. Bring a prepared lunch and several snacks. Some good snacks are fresh fruit, fruit leather, pieces of pared salad vegetables like carrots and celery, trail-mix, beef jerky, dried fruit, granola bars, or unsalted nuts. Trail-mix is a mixture of nuts, seeds (such as sunflower seeds), and raisins. Sometimes it includes small pieces of chocolate or carob. The simplest prepared lunch is sandwiches. Don't use eggs, mayonnaise, or salad dressing on sandwiches that are going to be without refrigeration.

If you are planning a hike for longer than a day, plan your meals very carefully. Make them pleasing, easy to prepare, easy to clean up, and light weight. The same kind of food that is sold in camping stores is also sold in your local supermarket, under commercial names and at much lower prices.

If water is no problem, you can get many dehydrated or freeze-dried foods that are easy to tote. You can purchase dry juice (Tang(c), for instance), milk, cereals, pancake mix, powdered eggs, spaghetti, macaroni, mashed potatoes and soups that are prepared with water.

You can purchase sauces and gravies, fruit drinks, spices, beans and lentils, and crackers. You can also buy canned meats and fish of all kinds, including chicken, sausages, meatballs, tuna, salmon, oysters, and so on. You can find combinations of both meat and pasta, or meat and vegetables, such as macaroni dinners, Chinese food, chicken and dumplings, spaghetti and meatballs, ravioli, and other canned or packaged dinners.

If you are planning to cook meals, observe the fire-making rules for the area in which you plan to hike. Fear of forest fires has created a need to change old-fashioned camping. Many hiking and camping areas request that you bring a portable stove for your cooking. Whatever your form of cooking, don't forget matches. Keep your strike-anywhere matches in a pill bottle or film container to keep them dry.

Carry flashlights with fresh batteries and extra batteries, as well.

Plan your trip completely before leaving home, and leave your itinerary with someone.

47
VISIT A POLICE OR FIRE STATION

Almost every child gets a chance to make a class visit to a police or fire station. But they usually don't get a chance to linger, look around, or ask questions.

Before just "popping in," call the station you want to visit and find out if you are welcome, and if so, the best time to come. If you live in the suburbs, country, or a small neighborhood, you may have a friend or two on the force. It's good for children to realize that police and firefighters are also parents and have children like themselves.

Find out if your local stations have films, talks, or brochures about child safety and preparedness. Plan to include these in your visit.

The officer in charge of these visits is prepared to talk to the children about his job without unduly frightening them. They will point out parts of the buildings that will be of the most interest. Don't expect to be taken to areas where the children will be in the way.

48
TRAIN STATION

There are still some beautiful old fashioned train stations in a few cities. Plan a visit to one of these stations for a morning trip.

Introduce the children to the inside of a train. Many train schedules allow a train to remain at a station for a few minutes to a half hour. Check the schedules for a train you can board, walk through, and then leave. See if you can show the children the bar car, a dining car, and a pullman sleeper.

Visit the central waiting room, luggage area, taxi-cab stand, information desk, and ticket sales windows. If your station has exhibits and displays, plan to spend some time examining them.

49
DOLL OR MINATURE MUSEUM

A doll or doll house museum is an historical collection in miniature. Both the dolls and the furniture represent a place and a time in the past.

If you examine the exhibits in their cases, you will find exact replicas of real furniture styles. Depending on the museum that you visit, you may find examples of historical greats in furniture production that are not duplicated in such detail and quantity anywhere else. Because most doll house or miniature collections are designed with such care and precision, they can represent the larger original version. Also, the rooms can display more than a regular museum exhibit because the space is used so effectively.

The displays exhibit not only the history of the doll itself, but also that of dress styles through the years. You will frequently find dolls representing famous people, from kings and queens to movie stars and space captains. These displays are as fascinating to boys as they are to girls.

Many miniature or doll museums contain collections of miniatures in transportation, agriculture, and, of course, warfare. There are frequently large exhibits of tin soldiers and army models.

50 COMPASS MYSTERY BUS TRIP

Go on a mystery bus trip. There are large commercially designed mystery bus trips for which you pay a fee and meet at a bus terminal. The driver has a hidden itinerary, and the passengers leave the terminal without any idea of where they are going. These trips can be fun.

You can plan an inexpensive version of this idea in your own town. Write the names of the four major compass points on four slips of paper. Let a child choose one. Start at a bus stop for your local bus, and travel in the direction dictated by the slip. Travel to the very end of the line. Plan to have lunch or a picnic at the destination.

Sit on the right side of the bus. Watch for all the sights that you can see from your bus window. At the end of your day, take a return bus and sit so that you can watch the other side of the street.

The next time you take a mystery trip, choose your direction from one of the remaining three slips of paper.

51 TELEVISION STUDIO

When you visit a television studio you may be surprised at how small it really is. Usually the audience is crowded and in an awkward position, unlike an audience at a play.

Many of the studios show visitors how they clue the audience to loudly clap at the appropriate time. Sometimes they exhibit the way old fashioned TV and radio programs made their sound effects.

Frequently, they take visitors to familiar program sets and point out familiar scenes. It can be fun to take this kind of a trip but be prepared for a lot of walking. If you want to take the children to a particular children's show (and there are still a few that have live audiences), you must make plans to get those tickets at least a year in advance.

52
SERVICE PROJECT FOR DISADVANTAGED KIDS

One of the best ways you can convince your children that they still have a pretty good life despite your divorce is to become involved with children who have fewer advantages.

Examine your own community to discover what needs you and your children can fulfill. There are many groups like Boy Scouts of America, Girl Scouts U.S.A., and the many "Y"s, that will be glad to accept volunteer help, as will the childen's school P.T.A. You and your children can be active in these groups together. You can find out whether your local Big Brothers/Big Sisters groups allows your children to participate in extending companionship to another child.

Find out the needs of local foster home agencies, orphanages, church groups, and hospitals. If you and your children can spend some time helping children who have less, they will learn how very much they truly have.

Special Occasions

There may be times when you can schedule a visit with your children for more than a weekend. Most frequently these times will come during their school breaks. School schedules are inflexible, so you will have to plan your vacation schedule to match the children's.

If the children's vacation comes at a time when you can't be completely free, then hire a baby sitter, "mother's helper," or paid-companion to be with them until you get home. Ask for, and check, the references for anyone that you plan to hire.

Plan your schedules in advance of the holidays. Make the plans with the children, not for them. Include some of the activities that they enjoyed in the past, and said that they would like to do again.

Vacation time is a time of rest and recuperation for children, as well as for you, their father. It is not necessary to always be "on the go." Enjoy at-home activities and lazy days. Enjoy seasonal activities.

TWO WEEKS EACH CHRISTMAS SEASON

Every winter holiday season in almost every city, there is a ballet performance specifically meant for an audience of children. Go see Tchaikovsky's Nut-Cracker Suite ballet--it's a children's fantasy with holiday spirit. Be sure to get tickets early in the season.

No matter what holiday you are celebrating, you can plan on making simple gifts for friends and relatives. Set aside several days for making and wrapping presents. If the children haven't made holiday presents for their grandparents, other relatives, and close friends, help them make inexpensive purchases now.

All of the stores are decorated and many have mechanical shows in their windows. Plan a day of window shopping. Wander through the stores and the malls, and look at all the holiday decorations. Visit Santa Claus. Don't forget to take your camera and color print film.

You can also plan to make holiday decorations like menorahs and tree ornaments. You can even make a wreath. If you live in the country, collect live evergreen or holly branches. If you live in the city, see if you can persuade the Christmas tree salesman to give you evergreen trimmings. You can make a wreath on a metal support or on a straw base. Both straw or metal forms are for sale in crafts shops. You can find books in the library or in crafts stores that contain ideas on how to make wreaths with tissue paper, crepe paper, ribbon, artificial fruit, and many other materials.

If you plan to buy a live Christmas tree, choose the tree with the children. If you are able to cut your own tree, wait until the children are with you to cut it. If you can afford to get a second tree for someone who cannot afford one, deliver it to them with the children. When you get your tree home, make a decorating party for yourself and the children. Serve cocoa and cookies, and share the decorating together.

Winter is a special time of the year for cold weather sports. Try downhill or cross-country skiing. Go sledding on trays, boards, or real sleds. Take a midnight sleigh ride. Go ice-skating indoors or outdoors. Make snow angels, a snow fort, snow and ice statues, or just an old-fashioned snowman. Take a winter hike or have a winter picnic.

Plan a holiday dinner with all the things that you all love best. Many restaurants and most large markets will cater a meal if you don't have the time or inclination to make it yourself. Plan also on spending some time visiting family.

TWO WEEKS EACH SUMMER

If you have the opportunity to spend two weeks or as much as two months with the children in the summertime, plan activities that lead into each other. For instance, on one day of your vacation you can take a ride to the country to see things growing. Watch for farm animals from the car windows. The next time, try to visit a farm or a farm zoo so that the children can see the animals up close, or even pet them.

Go bird- or bug-watching. Match the creatures you see to the illustrations in identification books. Try catching and raising a few tadpoles or a salamander. Get a book from the library to learn about the correct plants to include for a small animal terrarium.

Spend a day at the lake boating, fishing or swimming. To prepare for a day or afternoon of swimming, you have to plan for clothes (wet and dry), meals, towels, and toys.

If the beach, pool, or lake is near home, dress the children for swimming before you leave the house. Carry the dry clothes they will need in a sports bag. Don't forget underwear (or diapers). Carry a large plastic bag for the wet items. Include some kind of sandals for walking on hot sand or concrete.

If you will be at a very sunny or hot area, make sure everyone has a cap or sun bonnet. Don't allow the children to be exposed to the sun for too long. Keep them under an umbrella or in a protected area.

Use a sunscreen lotion on all skin areas, being careful to apply gently near the eyes.

Do not allow any young children to go near the water alone. Bigger and older children can accidentally knock over a small child, and the child can get both hurt and frightened.

Teach your children to never go near the water or go swimming without a buddy. Teach them to respond instantly to your call. Children can get very absorbed in playing and may not hear the first time you call. They may also respond to another parent calling a child with the same name. Develop a coded signal, perhaps calling their name twice, like "Jimmy Jimmy," or a whistle and then the name.

Feed the children at home, or immediately after you get to the beach or pool. In that way, you get the least sand or dirt mixed in with the meal, and you can get rid of the garbage immediately. Cleaning up quickly helps keep bugs away from your spot.

If the children have brought pails and shovels, use them for packing washcloths, bottles of water, and snacks.

Make your first trip a short one. Increase the length of the trip slowly as the children (and their skin) get used to the sun. Leave the beach before the children get too tired to walk under their own power.

3

AGES, INTERESTS, AND ABILITIES

Children of varying ages have different abilities and levels of skills. To enjoy your children, don't expect them to do more than they are actually capable of doing.

Children physically mature at different rates and not necessarily in ways that are recognizably matched by their abilities. For instance, by the age of two, the size, weight, and pupillary reflexes of the child's eyes are almost developed to those of an adult, but the child does not develop mature perception for quite a while.

Boys and girls of the same age and even the same size cannot do all tasks at the same rate. Little girls mature faster than boys in many ways. Some children remain awkward in certain skills longer than other children do, but sooner or later, most catch up.

This chapter will give you a very general idea of the range of a child's development for each age group, from infancy through adolescence. The variety of abilities that will be discussed include motor, language, visual, and perceptual skills, body awareness, hand manipulation and writing and reading skills, social and personality development, as well as areas that involve dexterity, patience, and perseverance.

You will see how one skill is built upon another, in an upside-down pyramid-type fashion, and how a new skill cannot be expected to appear until the earlier one is developed or learned completely. Realize that at certain stages during their growth it is not only perfectly normal for a child to take one developmental step forward and two backward, but that this backward appearing spiral in development is expected.

Although a developmental level is listed for one age, it can actually be bracketed by more, based on the rate of development of the child, particularly after four years of age. Throughout this section, (as throughout the entire book), the child is referred to as "he and him." Please consider that this reference is meant as he, she, him or her, and is used for convenience. Except where a specific sex needs to be referred to in a particular instance, the word "he" will always mean your child at that age.

Young children can get frustrated easily. They will walk away from an activity that they are not comfortable with. They get tired, bored, and cross when they are upset by not being able to accomplish what they are trying to do. Help them recognize their capabilities. Make sure that they can cope with the activity you plan. If they can't, discontinue it and do something else within their level. Examine a planned activity from many angles to make sure that it falls within the competency levels for your child. For example, a three-year-old child can go fishing, hold the rod, and recognize when a fish is biting, but a three-year-old cannot be expected to sit still for several hours.

Development takes place in many areas at the same time. The most noticeable is physical growth. You can observe this growth easily.

Clothes and shoes become too small. Arms and legs stick out of sleeves and pants, and hair needs frequent cutting. Teeth grow in, fall out, and are replaced with new larger teeth. Other areas of development are not quite as visible, but the changes are taking place.

INFANCY — The Stage From Birth Through 2 Years

Newborns

At birth, a baby doesn't seem to be able to do anything.

Actually, the baby is equipped with many reflex actions. A reflex is a response to stimuli. As the baby grows and develops actual skills, these reflexes are replaced with learned and more sophisticated movements.

Several reflex actions that are very obvious include the Moro, the startle, and the palmar grasp reflexes. Watch the baby as he lies on his back in the crib; when the infant extends his arms, fingers, and legs, and then draws them back close to his body, he is exhibiting the Moro reflex.

If the baby is surprised by a sound or a light being turned on, he will exhibit the startle reflex, which includes the flexing of the Moro reflex without the extension. It looks as though he baby is drawing into himself.

If you stroke an infant's palm with your finger or lightly touch the sole of his foot, you can observe the palmar and plantar grasp reflex. The baby closes his fist or curls the bottom of his foot as though he is trying to grab your finger.

The needs of a new infant are simple. The newborn baby needs feeding, cleaning, and cuddling. He needs a crib to sleep in, clean, dry clothes including diapers, and some visual stimulation. The infant also needs someone to get up at night to feed him and to soothe his small discomforts.

Hold the newborn baby in such a way that you are supporting his head with your hand or arm. His neck muscles are not strong enough to do the job without help.

By one month of age, the infant starts to exhibit the arm-supporting reflex and begins to look at objects. Seeing develops rapidly. At this age, he still does not need much more than the basic care discussed above. Hold him and talk to him. Be gentle; he is not ready for enthusiastic playing yet.

By the time your baby reaches three months of age, he can turn from lying on his back to his stomach. The baby truly starts enjoying visual experiences. At this age, he waves his arms in excitement when looking at objects. This is the age to make sure that many kinds of exciting visual stimuli are within his seeing area. If you put a collapsible crib in the corner of a room, attach a planter hook over the crib. Hang a mobile up when the baby visits; replace it with a plant when the crib is stored away.

Now that the baby can bring both hands in front of his body,give him a rattle to play with. At five months, the baby may place both his hands on his bottle. Put some brightly-colored toys near the baby and watch him as he begins to bring his hand to a toy as though he wants to take it.

6—Months

When the baby is a half-year-old, he stays up longer. He looks around a lot and enjoys having many things to see. Continue to supply the baby's viewing area with brightly-colored toys, pictures, mobiles, and crib toys.

At this age the baby starts mouthing objects and everything gets tasted. Become aware of all the areas that the baby can reach and clear away anything that may be dangerous. Watch out for small items like clips that might easily be overlooked when cleaning your home.

The six-month old baby begins to realize that you are aware of his actions, and he responds. Since the baby can grasp objects with his fingers, and shake, hit, or drop them, your response will dictate his response. Your baby learns that it is fun to drop toys and watch daddy pick them up. You can make dropping and retrieving your first real game together. The baby will enjoy the interaction, so listen for his cooing and laughing.

Ask your mother if she remembers at what ages you and your brothers and sisters started crawling. She'll probably respond with a different age for each of you. Nine months is the usual age at which most children creep or crawl, but some start earlier and some later.

Some babies exhibit the supporting reflex in the legs at about this age, and some can pull themselves up and walk along the edge of a piece of furniture like a couch, while holding on. If you hold his hands and support his weight, he may stand and try to walk.

Baby may say a word or two, and may even wave bye-bye. Make or get him a "busy-box" to play with. These toys, full of knobs, handles, push and pull levers, and brightly-colored pictures appeal on many levels. Check out the kind for each age level in the toy store. Use some of their ideas if you are making the toy yourself.

Make sure the paint you use on baby toys is lead-free and approved for use on children's toys.

1 Year Old

At one year of age, most babies can do a whole series of physical movements, including making the change from lying on their backs to the standing position. Many babies can walk with support. At one year of age, your baby is not the same helpless infant he was a few months ago.

He is developing finer hand skills at this age. If you put a crayon in the hand of a one-year-old, he will create aimless circular patterns on a sheet of paper. The baby can handle small objects and can put small objects into larger ones, like a button into a bottle. There are all kinds of commercial toys that use this concept, but you can create your own "put-this-into-that" toys by collecting a group of cups, bowls, short, fat bottles, empty juice cans, or paper clip dispensers. Use large buttons, dice, poker chips, or even carrot chunks for items to be inserted into the larger object. Watch while he plays to make sure that the button or small toy goes into the container and not the baby's mouth.

The one-year-old baby has developed an awareness of his self. He knows that he is the baby in the mirror. He watches his own hands, and is aware of his own movements. If two one-year old infants play side-by-side, you may notice a certain amount of rivalry for the toys.

By the time your baby has reached fifteen months of age, he is probably trying to creep up the stairs. By this age, the baby has learned to recognize words and pictures and will pat a picture in a book when you describe it, (for instance, "Where's the puppy?").

An 18-month old baby has simple food needs and likes holding his spoon himself. The baby can put cookies or crackers directly into his own mouth.

When your baby is 18-months old, he starts to name objects being held for him. He can specifically point to a picture in a book when he is asked to identify it.

The baby of this age can seat himself in a small chair by backing up to the chair and lowering himself into it. Now is the time to get push or pull toys. The baby enjoys that kind of activity, and also enjoys carrying large toys. Potty-training can now be seriously underway.

PRE—SCHOOL — 2—5 YEARS

2 Years Old

By the time your baby has reached two years of age, he is no longer completely dependent on you and can attempt to do almost everything a bigger child can do.

The "Terrible Twos" are not terrible to the two-year old, only to the surprised parent who is not prepared for the infant turning onto a child. The two-year old child feels capable of doing so many things at this age that he starts to test his own power. He tries to find out how much independence he has and how much he wants. He begins to examine his world of influence. He has discovered that he can say "No" just like daddy does. He may not even mean it, but he tries anyway. This is an exciting time to watch a child develop.

The two-year old enjoys his birthday party and having other children around but he is competitive.

The child who has started out with an awkward running-like walk gradually develops rhythm and his walking becomes smoother. His attempts at jumping are crude and he uses two feet. By the end of the year, he may even be able to walk sideways and backwards.

Your two-year old child can throw a small ball and use some play equipment. You can play some simple toss games using a ball or a bean bag and a wastebasket or laundry basket as the destination.

At this age, the child can play alongside another child.

The eyes of a two-year old are almost physically mature and are the size that he will have as an adult. He is now able to recognize complex concepts like the idea that the shapes of things don't change.

He can verbally identify some parts of his body and his face. He is past the "Where is your nose? Where are your toes?" stage. Now you can point to parts of his body and ask "What is this called?" and get the proper response.

The child can draw one or several lines which may cross. He is able to name the subjects in at least three pictures in a book.

Read to your child. Start a library of simple-worded picture books. You should also start a collection of children's records or tapes, including songs, rhymes, and stories. You will notice that the child responds to rhythmical sounds, and bounces, sways, and nods his head to the pleasing sounds.

3 Years Old

By the time that the child has reached three years, he has gained a great deal of balance and no longer has the awkward, baby walk. He can even walk a straight line (heel-to-toe) and hop two to three steps. A child of this age may be able to walk a balance beam for a short distance. A trip to the park should include a trip to the playground. The three-year old can enjoy and use the equipment.

The three-year-old child can throw a ball about ten feet. He responds physically to music. The child at this age becomes aware of his own performance. He will dance and act out the parts to a simple story.

The three-year-old has increased his ability to use writing tools and can draw a single cross, some patterns, and an enclosed space. He is able to identify four printed geometric forms like a square or circle. The child can actually play with another child of the same age.

The three-year-old can help you dress him and loves to undress himself.

Three is a fearful and an anxious age, and by the time the child reaches three and a half, you will notice a change in temperament, he has become very contrary. He may seem uncooperative and may even resist your help. Don't be upset by these changes; they are part of a child's developmental pattern and should be expected.

4 Year Olds

By the time your child is four years old, you can start planning real activities for the two of you. He is becoming physically adept and is able to do many things that he could not do before. But be careful not to plan activities that are still beyond his abilities.

A four-year-old can run smoothly and in good form and can walk a line drawn as the perimeter of a circle. The child can jump skillfully, walk a balance beam, and maneuver well on a tricycle. The four-year-old can completely feed himself.

Your child's drawings become more recognizable. He draws circles and squares. He draws crude figures, buildings, houses, and cars. He is even able to draw suns and faces.

He has a large vocabulary and loves having the

capability of speech. He enjoys whispering and sharing secrets. At this age, he enjoys playing in groups. You may begin to see unstructured competition between children.

At this age, the child becomes more involved with small, more precise activities which require greater manual dexterity. He identifies certain fingers and more parts of his body. He starts to recognize important capital letters. He uses a pair of scissors to try to cut a straight line. He laces his shoes and closes his front buttons.

The child of four develops new sophisticated fears like auditory fears (the sound of a machine starting or tree branches scraping the roof), as well as fears concerning old people, people of a different color, "bogeyman," and animals.

When the child reaches the age of four, you can readily see how growth factors affect even the personality traits of the child. At this age, you may experience things about your child that you would never foresee. For example, you can expect a four-year old to become selfish, rough, and impatient with his sisters and brothers.

The child of this age loves to hear a play on words and silly rhyming. He enjoys creating silly names of his own. Dr. Seuss books are very popular. He acts as though he has the power to control language. Your child may also exaggerate and tell tall tales. He probably also tattles a great deal and is boastful. As a matter of fact, he has learned to lie. The four-year old loves to watch adult reactions to the things he says and he might use profane or mildly obscene language.

Don't be surprised to hear your folks ask the question, "Where could he have heard those words?" Or you may get a phone call from your former wife asking the same question, unless, of course, you call and ask her first.

By four-and-a-half, the child is ready for many simple cut, paste, and color activities. He can match shapes in a puzzle board, simple jigsaw board, or a sticker book. He can examine any three items in a group and decide among them which is the biggest and which is the heaviest.

ELEMENTARY SCHOOL AGE —— 5—12 Years

5 Years Old

The five-year-old has gained many physical skills. He can broad jump 2-3 feet and can hop 50 feet in about 11 seconds. The five year old child can balance on one foot for almost five seconds and can catch a large ball that is bounced to him. He can ride a small bike with training wheels.

A five-year-old can distinguish between lateral, vertical, and horizontal lines. He can draw animals, trees, and airplanes. He has learned that there is a right and a left, but can't properly locate where they are.

At this age, three or more children can play together, and when they do, they establish and follow simple rules. Children of this age like to march to music and love parades. The five-year-old takes pride in certain possessions, as well as his personal appearance. They love "Show and Tell."

The five-year-old can recognize some important (to him) printed words. He also loves to be read to. He likes to color inside the lines, cut, paste, and mold things from clay. This is a wonderful time to begin doing arts-and-crafts projects together. The five-year-old builds rambling structures with blocks. You may want to introduce him to Lincoln Logs(R) and Lego(R) building sets at this time.

Five is a less fearful age, although there may be fear of the dark, thunder, and certain strange sounds. Your child may wake up with frightening dreams. Allow the child to have a night light --it will help him cope with his fears, and therefore, become in control of them.

A five-year-old becomes serious and poised. He depends on adult company and support and is cooperative. This is a very special time for grandparents. Their grandchild especially loves being with them, doing things together, and hearing their stories.

The five-year-old prefers his own home and yard to going out and yet he is very curious and eager for information. He asks questions in order to get information and then uses that information.

A five-and-a-half-year-old child likes to dress and undress dolls and play with a Tinker-Toy(R). He starts to lose baby teeth. This is a very emotional and tense age. The child may become very fearful and may complain of headaches and stomach pains. He may develop frequent colds and earaches.

6 Years Old

By six years of age, most children are in school. This is a very complicated time for many children. Up to this point they have spent their entire lives learning the rules of home and family. Now they must adjust to allow for the differences introduced in the school setting. Some children are not yet settled enough for sitting at a desk all day or for participating in other regimented activities. If your child seems unusually stressed or tense, you might want to find out how he is doing in school.

The six-year-old has probably improved his earlier skills. Now, he not only has learned about positions in space like up and down, and ahead and behind, but he can locate his right and left.

He can draw a triangle and make easily identifiable drawings. He accumulates odds-and-ends and enjoys his collections. The six-year-old loves to cut and paste paper, make three dimensional objects like baskets, boxes and books. Your child can probably print the numbers from 1 to 10 and may be able to count up to 20. The six-year-old loves to hammer, and this is a perfect time to start some simple carpentry crafts. Don't expect perfection, but do praise liberally.

The child of this age learns to skip and throw, using the proper weight shift and step.

Girls are superior in movement accuracy and boys become superior in forceful, less complex acts. From now on, you will be seeing more areas where boys and girls start to differ.

The children exhibit cooperative behavior, and in a small group, simple leadership patterns begin to emerge.. Your child's teacher may remark on this on his report card.

The six-year old is meeting a great number of children from different backgrounds in his school.

He is also probably enlarging the range of his neighborhood. He is hearing many stories about different lifestyles and other people's lives that he has been protected from until now. Some of these stories may become the cause of new fears.

He may develop a fear of the supernatural, large, wild animals, and large dogs. The new information he has gathered may lead to fear of the elements, of his parent's death, or even fear of being late to school. Don't be surprised that a six-year old becomes highly emotional.

He also can be expected to be boastful and to brag. He likes praise and approval while resenting correction. He is often rude, rebellious, and stubborn. The six-year old likes to dominate. He blames and criticizes others and is jealous of the possessions of others. Television is a great influence on the toys he wants.

The six-year-old starts having trouble dressing himself. He has difficulty choosing clothes. As a matter of fact, he has a hard time making up his mind about many things.

Despite all these negative sounding symptoms, the six-year- old can be most angelic, generous and companionable. The six-year-old likes table games that involve counting squares, using dice, and moving toy pieces around a board. He can understand the concept used in simple dominos. But be prepared, the six-year old likes to win.

Six-and-a-half is a much calmer age. Enjoy it because seven years is a much more serious age.

7 Years Old

The seven-year-old child can distinguish

between the lower-case letters, b, p, d, q. If he is still having difficulty with these letters, it might be a good idea to have him tested for any learning problems. The earlier these are diagnosed, the less frustrated the child becomes.

At seven, the child can draw a diamond, a figure quite different from a triangle. He can print several sentences, and repeat something he is doing over and over again.

The seven-year-old has acquired a great deal of physical dexterity and can balance on one foot while blindfolded. He can also hop and jump in small squares and walk a two-inch balance beam. Children this age participate in many of the sidewalk and street games that involve marking off play areas, and then hopping, standing, or jumping in them. They participate in games with complex rules and large groups. Their games and teams often include both sexes.

At this age, they participate in very vigorous activities and also in very passive ones. They exhibit more competitive behavior in their play.

The seven-year-old collects with a purpose. He likes to collect specific things at this age, and his choices for a collection are no longer as general. Because he can continue to sustain this interest, this is a good age to begin stamp or coin collections. Many youngsters show an interest in collecting miniatures. They will often take the opportunity to asking for an addition to their collection.

At seven years, the child becomes serious, absorbed, and thoughtful. He is empathetic to others yet this is also the age when he develops a "deaf" ear. (You might find that this ability to "turn off" his parents stays around throughout the teen years.) He will become annoyed with himself when he can't accomplish something the way he expects to.

His anger becomes self-directed, and he is often moody, sulky, and unhappy. He has developed visual and spatial fears. He has become aware of the larger world and now has fears of war, space, and burglars. He may fear that he is adopted and tests that theory with his friends. School is a great influence, and he develops fears about not finishing his work.

8 Years Old

At eight years of age, the child has fewer fears. He has less fear of weather and the elements. The eight-year-old tries to control his environment by being the teller of frightening tales. He compulsively repeats all the details of a fearful situation in order to bring it under control or to resolve it.

The eight-year-old is becoming more and more physically adept. Both boys and girls have a twelve pound pressure in their grip strength. Girls can throw a small ball forty feet, while boys can throw it farther. A child of this age can hop several times on one foot and alternate it with the same number of hops on the other. He can maintain this rhythmical hopping pattern. His body movements are also more graceful. He may enjoy taking piano lessons or learning a musical instrument.

The eight-year-old collects with zeal. He is very interested in the size of his collection. He can print all letters and numbers accurately.

At eight years, the child seems to take on life in a brave fashion, but often feels that he is being attacked. The child becomes impatient at this age, especially with himself. He is simultaneously demanding, fresh, rude, and strongly affectionate. The eight-year-old is very curious about other peoples' personal lives. He asks all kinds of personal questions, and listens in on phone calls and other personal conversations. He is critical of others and of himself. This age child can burst into tears or have a laughing jag. He has developed a sense of guilt, but, thankfully, he also has a good sense of humor.

9 Years Old

At nine years, boys can throw a small ball 70 feet. Girls can jump up 8-1/2 inches and boys can jump 10 inches.

They like to play in large teams in games with clearly-defined and rigid rules. Competition and cooperation is highly developed.

Nine-year-olds worry mostly about school failure. They enjoy frightening each other, and playing games that involve hiding or spying.

The nine-year-old works and plays hard (sometimes to exhaustion), and has an interest in his own strength.

He builds complicated structures with Erector(R) or Lego(R) sets and sketches and does detailed drawings. The nine-year-old is good with tools. Now is the time to begin the more complicated arts, crafts, and building projects you have been wanting to do together.

The nine-year-old is becoming more sophisticated. He can dress rapidly and has an interest in combing his own hair. The nine-year-old gets mad at his parents but also likes to brag about them. This is a more responsible age. The nine-year-old evaluates his own performance and may be ashamed of his past behavior. He wants things to be proper. The nine-year-old is protective and loyal to friends and younger siblings. Many complain of headaches and eye-aches. You may hear your child complain that his hand hurts when doing a task, but he still continues the task.

The nine-year-old enjoys humor and likes surprises in a story. He uses language to express subtle and refined emotion.

10 Years Old

The ten-year-old child can see and intercept a ball thrown from quite a distance. It is now possible for him to play in involved ball games and there is a real interest in structured team games. If you both are interested in little league games, now is the time to join. The children are now both physically and mentally able to participate.

The ten-year-old collects more formally, with specialized intellectual interest. Enjoy joining collector's groups with your ten-year-old. Many adult stamp, coin, photography and other specialty clubs will permit a child to join with a parent, if the child is serious about the interest.

The ten-year-old seldom cries and usually seems to be happy. The humor of a ten-year-old appears heavy and labored and not usually funny from an adult's standard. The child of this age does not seem to be able to take a joke on himself, but does a lot of punning, and enjoys riddles and practical jokes on others. He does not get angry too often, but when he does, it is violent, immediate, and expressed in physical terms. It is, thankfully, quickly resolved.

11 Years Old

When the child has reached eleven years of age, he has developed linear perspective. He also has greater physical ability and boys can jump five feet in the standing broad jump, while girls reach just six inches less. Sex differences are established in group organization and teams break into two groups, by sex.

ADOLESCENCE—12 Through 20–24 Years

Adolescence is a period of confusion and very strong emotions and the adolescent often feels frustrated, annoyed, under the control of others, being pushed around, incompetent, under-sexed, over-sexed, and generally miserable. The main school worries that children from ten to sixteen suffer concern homework, test-taking, and being unprepared for school. Some adolescents worry about their family's finances. Most want to be like their friends. They feel things in extreme degrees. They hate, love, are angry, and have feelings of isolation.

Adolescents are learning to recognize the extent of their own feelings and are afraid of feeling silly or appearing dumb. They worry about their own vulnerability.

You probably still have the parental ability to force your teen to do something that he is not familiar with, knowledgeable about, or comfortable doing. But hesitate before forcing him into a position in which he will feel inadequate. Many teen-parent arguments begin when a teen fears destroying his image or credibility. His self-image is very fragile at this age.

Teens worry about differences in their physical growth rate and they worry about their friends being disappointed in them. They worry about losing control and they are very self-conscious. They are both self-centered and unsure of their own identity.

Friends are extremely important to them. They are under a double assault of pressure from their peers and from the constant media blitz. They must make decisions about smoking, drugs, alcohol, sexuality, lying, and shoplifting. Adolescents get upset when their family finds fault with their friends, or considers those youngsters to be poor examples for them.

They have fears about many things they have no control over, like gangs, depravity, terrorists, and nuclear war.

While these tremendous stresses are forming their social maturity, they are still growing physically and in strength.

The twelve-year-old can now do a standing high jump of three feet, and the child of this age becomes aware enough to evaluate the outcome of a task. By thirteen years, the perception of body shape and performance capacity changes. Status is gained by boys in athletics.

The fifteen-year-old saves money with very specific goals in mind and shows an interest in money values. Frequently, the goals they save for may outrage a parent with a different set of values, who is scrimping and saving for that child's college tuition. Many teens work at odd jobs or babysit to earn money that they feel they should be able to spend freely with no explanation to a parent.

The older adolescent has achieved some control and awareness but may revert to an earlier and more disorganized stage when there are dramatic changes in his life, such as the divorce of his parents or the death of a family member or close friend. Exciting and positive changes, like going away to college, the marriage of a favorite brother or sister, or the remarriage of a parent can also cause him to revert to a more disorganized state.

The transition from adolescent to adult involves the resolution of conflicts by the adolescent himself. This transition requires the ability to feel fulfilled and to have created a self-identity. The adult feels less need for conflict to solve his problems, and he becomes more open to the give-and-take of normal living.

Footnote:
Perceptual and Motor Development of Infants And Children, Second Edition, Bryant J. Cratty University of California, Los Angles, Prentice-Hall, Inc., Englewood Cliffs, NJ 07632, 1979.

The Child From Five to Ten, Revised Edition, Arnold Gesell, M.D., Frances L. Ilg, M.D., Louise Bates Ames, Ph.d., Harper and Row Publishers, New York, Hagerstown, San Francisco, London, 1977.

4

CRAFTS, ACTIVITIES, AND MAKING THINGS AT HOME

All of the following crafts can be done in one form or another, to some degree, by most children. Have fun with your children and join in the activity. Enjoy finding out how talented your children may be. Have fun doing these at-home activities.

Most of these crafts will be fairly inexpensive and will use materials that you may already have or can easily get. Some of the projects can be finished at one sitting, while others may be continued for several of your children's weekend visits.

If you become very interested in doing these home crafts, you may find that you are saving things that used to be considered junk, like empty coffee cans, jars with screw-on lids, and scraps of fabric, buttons, and so forth. They provide the basic materials for most of these projects.

Cover your work area with several layers of newspaper, an old tablecloth, or an inexpensive painter's plastic drop cloth. If the children are very young or sloppy, cover the floor with newspaper, too. Wash or clean paint brushes thoroughly, squeeze them dry, and then stand them on their handles in a jar. If you are working with white glue, pour some in a jar lid or paper bowl, and use a stick for an applicator. You can even dip the edge of the object you are gluing right into the bowl. For controlled sanding of small objects, make a sanding block or use an emery board. An emery board is just rigid enough for a child to use.

Put finished projects in a safe place to dry. If you have to spray paint anything, put it into an open carton, so that the bottom of the box becomes the back, and the sides of the carton confine the spray.

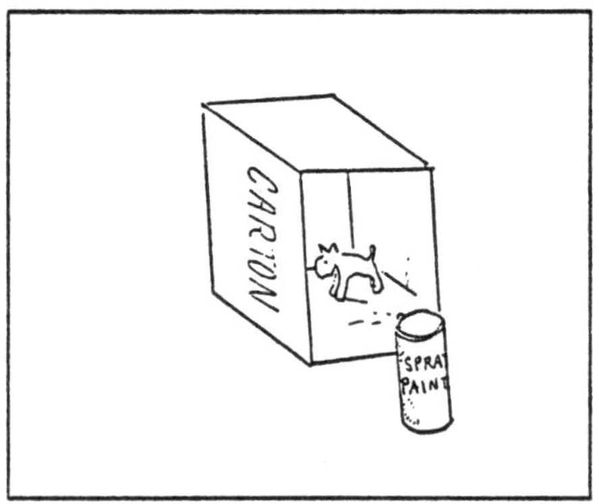

Making Things at Home

MOSAICS AND COLLAGES

A mosaic is a picture or decoration composed of small pieces of one particular type of material. Most often, mosaics are made of small pieces of stone, gems, or tile.

A collage is a picture made up of small pieces of many different materials, including stone, tile, paper, magazine pictures, leather, metal, plastic, feathers, and anything else that can be glued to a backing.

WHAT YOU NEED: You can use paper as a background on which you glue very light material, or use cardboard, part of a carton, or a piece of wood for heavier collages or mosaics. White glue is usually adequate for most materials.

Collage material can be any of the items mentioned above, as well as buttons, toothpicks, marbles, stamps, tokens, pictures cut out of catalogs, scraps of all kinds, and so on.

Mosaic materials should be the same three dimensional material in different shapes, colors, or textures. Different shapes of pasta or macaroni make a delightful mosaic, as do broken colored egg shells, seeds, or dried beans.

WHERE TO GET MATERIALS: Garage and tag sales are a great place to buy junky old jewelry to break apart for beads, stones and "gems." Some fabric stores sell scraps and remnants. A walk at the beach, shore, or park can provide a whole collection of pebbles and shells (both broken and whole). Save scraps left over from other crafts and activities in a paper bag called the "Scrap Bag."

DIRECTIONS: A rainy day, or a day when a child has a cold or you are tired, is a good day to pull out the collection of scraps and start a collage. A collage can be made with no preparatory drawing. Just glue one item next to another onto the backing. You can leave spaces or partially touch one piece of material with another. You can construct a picture or a decoration. It can be a real representation or a fantasy. You can draw a picture first, if you wish, and then complete it with the collage effect.

If you are planning to make a large or heavy collage or mosaic, or one that may be mounted as a wall decoration, use a board as the backing. Stain or paint the board ahead of time. Finish it with a coat of polyurethane or shellac.

To make a mosaic, start with a simple line drawing of the picture. Pictures in coloring books are excellent guides for outline drawings. Divide the material you are using by color. If you are using pebbles or small rocks, wet them to see their real color. Then glue the material pieces into the spaces of the drawing, one piece right next to the other to create an area of color. Create a curve rather than a straight line, in some areas. Fit odd shapes together like a jigsaw puzzle. When the mosaic is finished, spray it with polyurethane. You might need a second coat to make the color of pebbles and stones show up better.

VEGETABLE PRINTS

Another at-home craft is making vegetable prints. A teenager or an adult should do the cutting on this project.

WHAT YOU NEED: You will need a piece of firm root vegetable and a paring knife for each person. A potato works best because it is the easiest to hold, but you can use Jerusalem Artichokes, carrots, or turnips as well. You will also need colors or dyes, and paper. You can make the colors from vegetable coloring diluted in water (you can find these in the baking section of the market), poster or acrylic paints, or use stamp pads. For paper, use drawing paper, blank newsprint, shelving paper, old stationery, or paper bags cut open and flattened.

DIRECTIONS: Cut a potato in half, and then, using a pencil or a nail, draw a simple shape on the cut side of one of the potato halves. Use a paring knife to cut around the outside edge of the shape. Cut away about 1/4 - 1/2 inch of excess vegetable, so that the shape is raised from the surrounding surface.

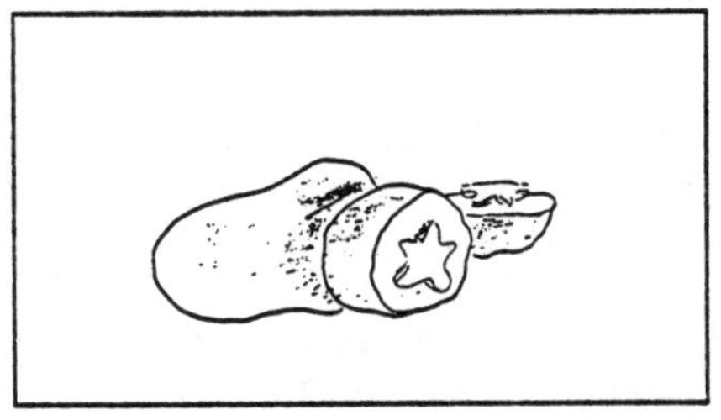

Make a different shape on each vegetable. Dip the vegetable into the color or press it onto the ink pad. Then, press the stamp on the paper. Make a repeat pattern of the various shapes.

Vegetable prints make nice greeting cards, decorations, or logo-style imprints for children's stationery.

Throw the vegetables away after using them for making prints; they are no longer good for eating, and can't be saved to be used again for making prints.

BUBBLE SPACE CITY

Save the clear, rigid, plastic packaging that surrounds small purchases. You will often find shaving and cosmetic items with this kind of blister-pack on hanging displays. Also keep the cardboard backing until you are ready to start your project. When you have collected a quantity of bubble packages, you can start to make a town.

WHAT YOU NEED: You need the empty bubbles, glue, paint and brushes. Acrylic paint sticks to the plastic and tube acrylics even come in silver, copper, bronze, and gold. You may need scissors. You will also need cardboard from a carton or a gift box.

WHERE TO GET MATERIALS: The paints can be purchased in an art, hobby, or hardware store, or the art section of some department stores.

DIRECTIONS: Design a base for the city from the cardboard carton or gift box bottom or lid. Decorate the base so that it is correct for your space city. Arrange the bubbles until you have them positioned the way you want them. Draw a light outline around the shapes on the base. Paint the buildings with the acrylic colors. When they are dry and ready to be glued down, set them aside. Spread a thin line of glue on the base, just inside one of the pencil outlines. Set that building on the glue. Carefully glue each bubble building to the base in its proper place.

Allow the entire bubble city to dry completely. If you wish, add pebbles, rocks, pictures, or drawings.

SOAP—CARVING

After a visit to a museum, everyone may be inspired to try sculpting.

Soap-carving is fun and mistakes can easily be corrected by using water to glue parts together. When the carving is all done, the scraps can be used for washing.

WHAT YOU NEED: Soft white soap like Ivory (R) makes the best carving soap. You can get small or large cakes of soap in the supermarket. Start out with big cakes.

You will need a simple drawing or picture for a pattern, that is almost the size of the cake of soap. Don't plan anything with delicate detail. Animal shapes that are bulky like seals or bears are good subjects. You will also need a paring knife and a butter knife for carving and a pencil or carpenter's nail and fork for scribing.

DIRECTIONS: Scrape the brand name off the large side surfaces of the soap with the butter knife. Lay the pattern on the soap and scribe the design, with the large nail or a sharp pencil, on one large surface. Reverse the pattern on the opposite side of the soap so that it makes a left and right side, both facing the same direction and lined up with each other. Scribe this pattern on the soap.

Taking very small chips, cut away the excess soap from the pattern. Use warm water on your hands to smooth rough parts. When the soap is almost dry, use a fork to make designs on the shape, or to draw fur.

BUILD A BIRD HOUSE OR FEEDING STATION

If you live in the suburbs or country, build a birdhouse to mount on a pole or hang from a tree. If you live in the city, build a bird-feeding station to mount on the outside of a window sill.

Before starting to build it's a good idea to know what kind of birds frequent your area. Birds are known to favor one kind of house over another. If you are building a birdhouse, build an appropriate one. Check the library for bird books or buy a pocket-sized edition of a bird book. You can also use it for bird-watching when you go camping.

WHAT YOU NEED: You will need birdhouse plans. The books mentioned above usually contain patterns for each design plan. Lumber yards often have packages of birdhouse patterns.

You will need carpentry tools such as a hammer, saw, and nails and possibly a screwdriver and wood screws. You may need sandpaper, paint, and a brush. If you paint the birdhouse, you will need paint cleanup materials.

WHERE TO GET MATERIALS: In addition you'll need wood and trimming materials. Some lumberyards have a scrap box. The scrap box often contains pieces large enough to work with, but the wood costs only pennies or nothing at all. If you buy a large piece of wood, the lumberyard might cut it into smaller pieces following your directions, as a service.

Obviously, you have to do some research ahead of time for this activity. It might be a good idea to prepare the materials after a trip to the bird section of the zoo or after a camping/bird-watching trip.

DIRECTIONS: A feeding station doesn't have to be any fancier than an ordinary shelf. Add upright edges to the shelf to keep the seeds from scattering. Make sure there are some drip holes so that neither rain nor snow fill the shelf. Use a couple of L-brackets to balance the shelf against the building and straight brackets to attach it to the window sill.

If you know someone who knits or sews, collect thread and wool scraps, and stuff them into a mesh bag (the kind onions come in). Hang the bag near the shelf or birdhouse. The birds will enjoy the nesting material.

PAPER—MACHE and SAWDUST MACHE

Both paper-mache (papier-mache) and sawdust mache are made with scrap material, water, and paste which, when combined, may be used to create permanent and attractive decorations. Plan this activity to take several weeks, since you have to allow the mache to dry thoroughly between applications.

WHAT YOU NEED: To make sawdust mache you need wheat-paste and, of course, sawdust. Sandpaper can be used to smooth a finished piece of work. You can use paint to decorate the dry sculpture, but the natural finish often looks very nice. To make paper-mache, you need wallpaper paste or wheat-paste, newspapers, and material to form a base for the shape.

WHERE TO GET MATERIALS: You can get the wheat-paste in dry form in a hardware or in a paint-and-wallpaper store. Save odds and ends such as cardboard, material, and Styrofoam to use in these projects. Also, you will need a large quantity of newspapers, including the colored comic section.

DIRECTIONS: To make sawdust mache, mix a cup of sawdust with a cup of prepared wheat-paste. Stir them together into a thick, sticky consistency. Add water sparingly if necessary. Use your hands to make a baseball-sized lump. Press and mold the sawdust mache into a shape. Use handy kitchen tools, nails, and sticks to press features into the wood mix. When you are pleased with the results, allow it to dry thoroughly. When the statue is all dry, you can sand it if necessary, or paint and decorate it.

Paper wet in thin, wheat-paste can be arranged on an armature or base to make a paper-mache object that is permanent and interesting. The process is simple--tear newspapers into strips or cross-tear the strips into squares. Pile all the black newsprint strips in one pile and all the color print in another. Prepare the wheat-paste as directed on the box. Dilute the paste in a one-to-one mix, and then stir it well.

Several suggestions follow for decorations. Paper-mache becomes very solid when it is dry, and can actually be used for furniture.

A Styrofoam(R) Plaque:

Collect the Styrofoam(R) forms that surround radio and electronic components. Glue them to a board. When all the base parts are glued down, add another level of styrofoam pieces to create greater dimension. Dip the black-and-white news-print strips into the paste and squeeze the excess water out by pulling it between two fingers. Drape the wet paper over the styrofoam. Keep adding pieces of glue-wet paper, until the entire shape and board are covered. When there is no space or foam showing through, start all over again, but this time use the colored strips. By alternating color print and black print you can tell if you have skipped any areas.

Allow the paper-covered board and foam to dry thoroughly. It might take a week. Repeat the process, adding two more layers of paper, then if necessary repeat again. When the paper is completely dry, spray paint the plaque. You can use a metallic spray or plain white. Use a darker color of metallic paint or a bright primary color on various surfaces and faces of the plaque. When dry, spray the entire surface with polyurethane. Frame the plaque and hang it as a wall decoration.

Fruit Shaped Bowl:

Blow up a large, round balloon using one that is a little larger than an adult's head. Using black newsprint paper, cover the entire balloon with paper-mache. Apply a second coat using the colored newsprint. When the paper-mache is completely dry, examine the shape. If the fruit that the bowl should resemble has a different shape from the ball you have made, glue or tape balls of dry, crushed newspaper to the appropriate places. Build up the top of an apple or add a small ball to the top of a big one to get a pear shape. Add the next two layers of paper-mache, smoothing the additions into the shape you want. Allow the paper-mache to dry. Using a hand saw or an old steak knife, cut one-third of the top off the shape. Pull out the balloon and allow the entire bowl to dry. If necessary, use more strips to finish any incomplete areas. When totally dry, paint the bowl and the cover (inside and out) with acrylic paints in the colors associated with that fruit. Add some highlighting colors. When the paint is completely dry, spray with polyurethane.

Statue:

You can make a primitive animal statue by

building an armature of folded newspaper held in shape by string.

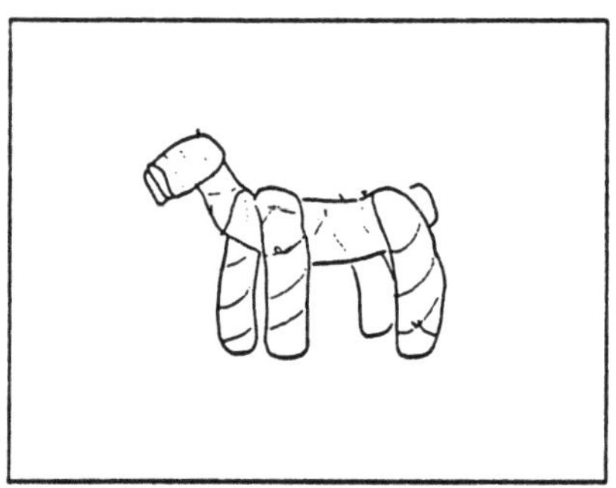

Wrap the strips of newspaper around the shape, using a layer of each color of newsprint, as before. Allow the layers of each color of newsprint to dry thoroughly. Add small squares of paper-mache to build up the face areas. Form a forehead, muzzle, ears, eye shapes, and so on. Form shoulder and leg muscles. Add paper wherever it is needed and allow the animal to dry. When it is all dry, paint the body. Then add features. You can use buttons for eyes, string for a tail, and straw for whiskers.

NATURE CREATURES

Making animals, people, and other creatures from objects found in nature can be fun to do after a trip. It's a quiet activity that can help the children unwind after a busy day.

WHAT YOU NEED: Like most of the other projects described in this chapter, this one also uses scrap materials like paper, cardboard, string, pipe-cleaners buttons, toothpicks, wool, and thread. It also requires white glue and acrylic paints. You'll also need the natural materials you can find in a park, the beach, your yard, or on a trip. Collect shells, rocks, pebbles, small sticks, driftwood, pods, nuts, and pine cones.

Combine the natural and scrap materials to make creatures or scenes. Paint any special effects that you want to create.

PLASTER OF PARIS PRINTS

You might want to practice using this material before going on a camping trip. Then you will know how to use it for making prints of real tracks.

WHAT YOU NEED: You need plaster of Paris (you can get it in a hardware or paint store), an old bowl that you can mix the plaster in, and something to stir with. You also need water to make the mix, an object to make a print of, and a few paper clips.

Some sort of material to confine the plaster when you are making a print is also necessary. You can use cardboard, an empty tuna fish can with both lids removed, a plastic bleach container, and so forth.

DIRECTIONS: There are several kinds of prints that you can make. If you are pouring the wet plaster into a track or paw print in sand or dirt, the print that results will be raised. If you are laying a leaf or your hand on the plaster and then removing it, the results will be depressed. If you arrange pebbles and shells on wet plaster and allow them to dry into the plaster surface, the effect will be three-dimensional.

To create a border around a paw print or track in the dirt, bend a strip of cardboard or plastic cut from a bleach bottle into a circle, and clip the edges together. Scratch a groove in the dirt or sand, and stand the circle in the groove. If it is a small print, you can use the empty tuna can. Coat the insides of the can or plastic from the bleach bottle with vaseline before using it. Prepare the plaster and pour it into the track. Add enough plaster to fill the area around the track up to the border of the plastic ring. Allow it to dry very thoroughly. Plaster of Paris gets quite warm while it is curing. Wait until it is cold before you try to lift it.

To make a depressed print plaque, choose a perfect green leaf. It must be green to be flexible enough to press evenly against the plaster.

Use an old container like a plastic bowl or the cut-off bottom of a bleach container to hold a small quantity of the plaster of Paris. This time you are using the plastic for a mold. Use petroleum jelly to coat the inside of the plastic container. Lay a paper clip on the bottom of the container, and then pour plaster of Paris to a height of an 1-1/2 to 2 inches. Before the plaster starts to set, arrange the leaf on its surface, pressing the veins and the stem into the surface.

After the plaster has cured and cooled, peel off the leaf. Remove the mold from the container. Pull the clip partially away from the plaster and use it to hang the plaque up later. The leaf shape or the entire plaque can be painted and sprayed with polyurethane to preserve it.

Homemade Finger—Paints

Finger-paints could also be called hand-paints, wrist-paints, and arm-paints. Finger-paints are very sloppy, so make sure there is lots of paper on the work area, even if there is plastic protecting it. The newspaper will absorb some of the moisture. Even a very young child (not an infant) enjoys the gooey feeling of finger-paints. Watch very young children when doing any activity--there is a tendency to taste everything. They also shove small items in their nose and ears. If you older child likes crafts activities but the younger one gets in the way, wait until nap time, or put the baby in the crib or playpen.

WHAT YOU NEED: You will need a box of cornstarch, water, a stove, and a pot to boil the mixture in. You can also use oil of wintergreen to keep the paints from spoiling, food colors to tint the paint, soap flakes to make a smoother texture, and lidded jars to keep the prepared paints in.

DIRECTIONS: Mix 1/4 pound of cornstarch into just enough cold water to dissolve it. Bring two quarts of water to a boil and then lower the flame to a simmer. Pour cold starch into the boiling water, stirring constantly--it thickens immediately.

If you wish, you can add two cups of soar flakes or a few drops of oil of wintergreen. When the mixture cools, divide it into several jars and add one color to each jar. Don't make too many colors.

Use the least expensive, glossiest white shelving paper (or other shiny paper) for finger-paint ing. Tear off an 18 inch strip and put it on the table, glossy side up. Put a tablespoon of water on the paper and spread it all over. Put two o* three tablespoons of finger-paint in the center of the paper and let the child spread it around.

Finger-painting is usually done in one color The tints and hues that express color are achieved by making the paint solid, allowing it to thin out, or letting white paper show through. Use the fingers, hands, side of hands, wrists, or arms to press, draw and swirl the paint on the paper.

When the picture is dry, use it to decorate a book cover or an empty large can. You can also use the finger-painting to decorate the child's possession box (see Chapter 6).

DECOUPAGE

Another way to decorate a child's possession box, a wooden box, piece of furniture, or a board is with decoupage. Decoupage is an activity that must be continued for many weeks, and as a result, you will again have the opportunity to develop a sense of continuity. It will help him feel that there is something specific to do when he visits. A continuing activity will help him to feel that your home is his too.

WHAT YOU NEED: You'll need a firm backing for the decoupage. If you use a board, wooden box, or a piece of furniture, first sand the wood, and then stain or paint it the color you want. Collect magazine pictures with a theme. For example, if you are decorating furniture for a collector of cars, use car pictures. If a child likes birds or flowers, use pictures with those kinds of subjects. Gather enough pictures to completely cover the surface of the backing material, making sure there are enough pictures to overlap each other.

You will also need glue, scissors, shellac, alcohol, and a brush. Use the alcohol to clean the shellac brush. Shellac comes clear and orange. The orange gives an antique effect.

DIRECTIONS: Neatly cut out all the pictures. Glue them to the wooden or heavy cardboard surface, and allow them to dry completely. Brush shellac completely over the whole surface going only from left to right. When the shellac is dry, brush another coat over the surface, going from top to bottom. Keep brushing layers of shellac on the surface, alternating the directions of the strokes and allowing each layer to dry thoroughly between applications. When you have applied enough shellac to the surface and you can no longer feel the edges of the pictures, add two additional layers of shellac to the pictures and to the rest of the box or furniture.

LEATHER CRAFTS

Working with leather is another craft that can continue from week to week. Activities in leather are interesting to children, teens, and adults. A simple interest in lacing can grow into leather-crafts like carving leather.

This activity takes preparation and the purchase of materials. Spend some time looking through a hobby store or a leather crafts catalog before making choices. Start very simply, perhaps with a laced change purse or a belt made of interlocking pieces of leather.

Leather craft stores may have some free patterns to use with leather. They also have pattern books. Teach the children to keep their tools sharp, clean, and in a rack.

CAR TOWN

WHAT YOU NEED: To make a car or boat town, you need a medium-sized cardboard carton with all four sides and the bottom in good condition. You'll also need paint or crayons and a collection of natural objects like small stones, pebbles, and sticks. You'll also need a saw or a strong knife to cut the box, and a length of rope or very heavy cord. Add some glue to the list of items you need.

DIRECTIONS: Cut the sides of the box away from each other so that the box can lie flat. Do the cutting neatly, so that you can fold the sides up again and tie them back into a box with the rope.

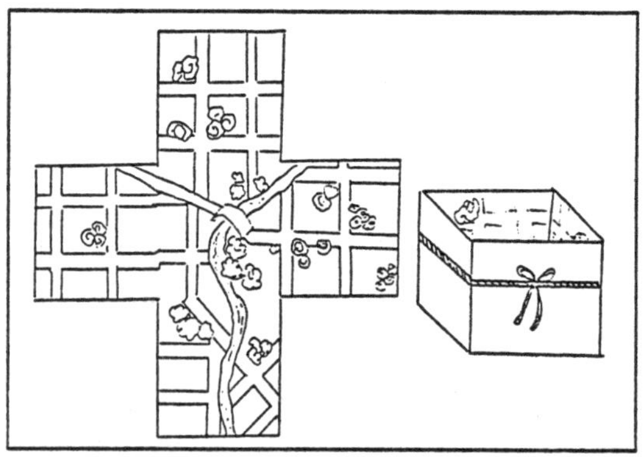

With the box in the open, flat position, design a town. Draw the roads. Glue pebbles to the box. Create bridges from cardboard or small boxes. You can use paper-mache to build bridges. You can also make hills with the paper-mache. For trees, use small twigs, pressed into clay or stuck into the box. Paint blue rivers. Have the road cross the river over a bridge. Small milk and whipping cream cartons can become buildings. Use acrylic paint on the waxy surface or glue paper around the cartons. Paint flowers in the park areas.

Run tiny cars or small boats over the town roads and rivers. Store the cars and boats as well as the carton houses, and so forth, in the box. Fold the sides up and tie the box into its original shape with the rope.

DIORAMAS

Another project to make in a box is a diorama. Consider this activity after visiting a zoo, aquarium, or museum, where the children see exhibits in stage-like settings.

WHAT YOU NEED: You will need an empty shoe, tissue, or carton box, a needle and thread, some pipe cleaners, scissors, paints and brushes, and your scrap bag.

DIRECTIONS: A diorama is a three-dimensional exhibit that has a defined background, and middle area. The children can draw the background on paper and press it into the box, or draw on the inside of the box itself. If a drawing on paper is used, curve the paper as it is inserted into the box, rather than pressing it into the corners. The curve gives greater dimension by creating the feeling of distance. Pictures can be drawn or cut out of magazines and pasted onto the backdrop. Make the background pictures smaller than similar objects in the foreground.

String the pictures, drawings, or three-dimensional objects on thread. Use a needle to push the thread through the bottom and top of the box in the middle ground area. Knot and glue the thread to the box. Glue free-standing objects to pipe cleaners to give them stability. Press them into the box bottom in the foreground. Add wings to birds or airplanes, fins to fish, and petals to flowers, to give a three-dimensional effect.

PUPPETS

Dolls and figurines representing real life can very often be the ideal medium for an unhappy or disturbed child to verbalize his frustrations, hurts, and angers.

Many psychologists use dolls and puppets in analysis and treatment. Even a "normal," stress--free child exhibits the freedom to playact his fears through puppetry.

If you and your children decide to make puppets, allow them to put on a show for you. Their puppet show will probably be amusing and charming, but it may also give you some insight into their thinking during this often troubled time that you are sharing.

Puppets have forms that range from the two-dimensional shape of stick and shadow puppets to three-dimensional sock, finger, and hand puppets, and the string puppets called marionettes.

Sock puppets can be made to cover the whole hand with a mitten-like covering that creates a mouth. These are the easiest for a very young child to manipulate. Hand puppets cover the hand and are controlled by the thumb and next two fingers. These puppets can hold or grab things, and can have a head shape posed on the pointer finger.

Sock Puppet Hand Puppet

WHAT YOU NEED TO MAKE A SOCK PUPPET: Use an adult-sized sock that covers the child's hand loosely, but not limply. Gather a collection of scraps from the scrap bag that can be used for eyes, ears, hair, whiskers, tongue, and jewelry or neckwear.

DIRECTIONS: Mold the sock over the child's hand, so that the sock forms a mouth. Indicate the locations of eyes, nose, ears, and so forth with a pencil or marker. Remove the sock from the hand and put it over a jar or can. The child can sew or glue the eyes in the proper places. Add other features. When everything is dry, you can play with the puppet. If the child is not too young, he may be able to sew a piece of cardboard into the bottom of the mouth portion to make the lower jaw match the top in shape.

WHAT YOU NEED TO MAKE A HAND PUPPET: Cut a gingerbread cookie-shaped person from cloth. The shape should have a large head, two arms, and a dress-like body. Use a piece of paper for a pattern for the cloth puppet body.

DIRECTIONS: Have the child spread his hand in a forced "T" on the paper (extending the thumb and middle-finger away from the pointer finger). Draw around the fingers in a loose, curved design, using the fingers as a general guide to the shape. Fold the paper in half and cut a shape that evens out the difference in the two halves of the drawing. Make the space around the pointer finger extra wide. Leave extra room on the edges to sew or glue the fabric together. Fold a piece of fabric in half. Pin or staple the pattern to the material and cut through both pieces. Remove the pins, staples, and pattern, and turn the material so that the two right sides face each other. Sew or finish the sides and turn the puppet body right side-out. It should look like a three finger glove.

Draw or paint features on the part that is held upright by the pointer finger. You can stuff some fabric scraps or cotton balls into the head to round it out. If you are using a paper-mache head, cut off the tip of the fabric that covers the pointer finger and attach the fabric to the paper-mache head. Use a small rubber band around the material and the neck to form a turtleneck collar.

If you want to add a head form to a hand puppet, you can purchase a doll head in a hobby and craft shop, or you can make a head from paper-mache.

To make a paper-mache head, follow the papier-mache instructions given earlier for making a fruit bowl. This time use a petroleum jelly-coated, burned-out light bulb for the base. When the basic head shape is dry, cut it off the light bulb. Use an old steak knife or a hacksaw blade to cut a line from the base of the bulb up and over the top and down the opposite side to the base. Allow the inside to dry and then glue the halves together. Prop the head on a broom handle or other dowel and seal the glued edges with paper-mache. Add other features to the head with small pieces of paper-mache.

Make sure that the neck is reinforced with strips of paper-mache. When it is thoroughly dry, paint the whole head. Complete the puppet by adding hair and features.

MOBILE

A mobile combines objects, balance, and air movement to create a pleasurable decoration. An attractive mobile is fascinating and can be hung from the ceiling of any room.

WHAT YOU NEED: You will need a plant or cup hook for the ceiling, several wire clothes hangers, thread or fish line, and several objects to balance.

Choose objects to hang from the mobile that look appropriate in the air--like miniature model airplanes, kites, or hot air balloons. Birds, balloons, bubbles, and butterflies look good, too.

Use a theme for a mobile that will hang in a child's room. You can use zoo animals, nursery-rhyme characters, or garden flowers.

Older children and teens can make light-weight wood or plastic models or origami. Younger children can glue cutout pictures or commercial stickers to cardboard or meat-tray Styrofoam.

DIRECTIONS: Use wire clippers to cut three different lengths of wire from wire hangers. Use needle-nose pliers to bend a closed loop at both ends of all three wires. Bend a gentle curve in each wire. Try to notch the center of each curve with your pliers.

Use a needle to thread an 18 inch length of thread or fishline through the top of any soft objects you plan to hang. Glue the thread to the top of stiff or rigid objects. Tie the other end through the loop at the end of the wire. You may want to adjust the length of the hanging thread after the mobile is hung.

Lay the three wires on a table, keeping them parallel to each other and about six inches apart. Use a very strong thread or fish line to join the wires at their center notches, starting with the bottom wire. Leave a long thread attached to the top wire, so that it can be looped and hung from the hook.

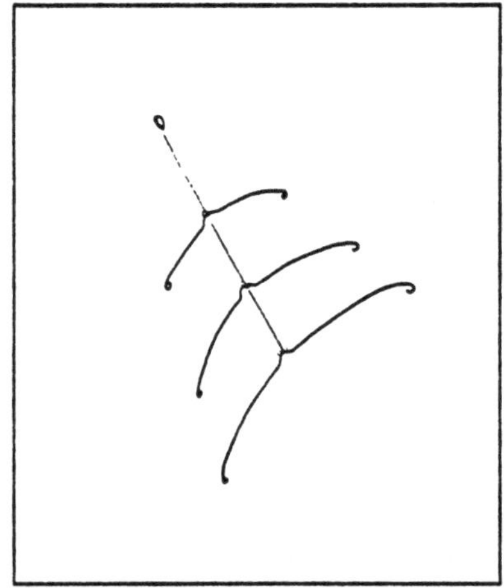

When the mobile is hung, you can adjust thread lengths so that the objects balance and away in the air currents.

SWISS CHEESE CANDLES

You can make candles the old fashioned way by dipping, or use metal molds to create commercially acceptable ones. You can add pressed leaves and flowers to candles or make a sand mold for free-form designs. Candles can be formed, colored, and scented and can use many different kinds of wicks. The following plans are for a very simple but interesting candle.

WHAT YOU WILL NEED: You will need an old, tall candle. It won't matter if it is broken as long as the halves stay together. You will need several blocks of refined paraffin, which you can find in hobby stores or the canning section of the market. You will also need an empty one-quart cardboard milk container, an empty coffee can, and an empty tuna can. You will need at least two to four trays of ice cubes. You can make either an uncolored candle or you can color it with chunks of crayon or wax dye. You must have hot mitts or pot holders handy.

DIRECTIONS: The empty coffee can is going to be used as the top part of a double-boiler. Wax that is in the process of melting is very flammable. Therefore you melt it by the double-boiler method, keeping the wax away from direct heat. Place the upside-down tuna can in the bottom of a large pot. Stand the coffee can on the smaller can. Break up a block of wax and put it in the coffee can. Pour water into the large pot to a height one-third up the outside of the coffee can, keeping the wax dry. Bring the water to a slow boil, keeping a constant watch on the melting wax. Never let a child melt wax or make candles without adult supervision. When the wax is melted, turn the heat off.

If you want a colored candle, stir the wax coloring or pieces of crayon into the melted wax. Use only one crayon color so that the candle will be a single color. To make this candle look like cheese use yellow coloring. You can experiment with mixing colors another time.

Remove the ice cubes from the trays. Stand the candle up in the empty milk carton. Pack the ice cubes all around the standing candle so that they support it and the candle can stand erect by itself. Pack enough additional ice cubes into the carton to reach the top. Reheat the wax to the bubbling point. As soon as it is heated, lift it carefully from the pot of water, using pot holders or mitts. Carefully pour the liquid wax over the ice cubes. Keep pouring until the wax reaches the top of the carton. Tap the side of the container twice gently to help move the wax through the entire carton. After the wax has hardened and cooled, carefully peel the carton away from the candle. Set the candle on a plate if you plan to burn it.

INDIAN BEAD PENDANTS

Indian jewelry is fun to make and wear whether your child is a boy or girl. Many of the western American Indian designs are geometrical while the eastern American Indians often use floral motifs in their designs. Before making the bead pendants, decide which kind of design you want to use.

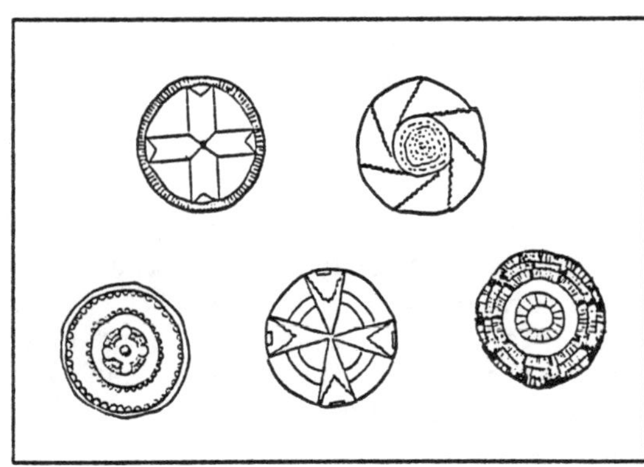

WHAT YOU NEED: You will need several plastic tubes of Indian beads, each in a different color. Be sure to get at least one tube of white. These beads are available in hobby stores, craft centers, and some sewing stores. You will also need a disk to glue the beads to. A disk can be cut out of wood or heavy cardboard. If you use cardboard, draw around a juice glass to make the circle. You can use the plastic or metal tops from frozen juice or refrigerated biscuit cans or you can purchase flat, round wooden disks, as well as other shapes, at hobby and craft centers. Purchase a pin-back or jewelry loop at the same place. You will also need the kind of white glue that dries clear.

DIRECTIONS: Draw an outline of the design in the center of the disk. Dab a little glue in the center, and start applying the beads. Arrange the beads so that their stringing holes don't show. Press one bead tightly to the next, filling the spaces. Form a curve with the beads in rounded areas. Fill in the entire disk face.

When the pendant is dry, glue the pin-back or loop to the back of the disk. The disk can be hung from a length of leather strip, or the remaining Indian beads can be strung on thread or dental floss and used as a necklace with the pendant hanging from the middle.

STRING ART

String art is an art form that older children, teens, and adults can enjoy. It is precise art and requires the use of compasses, protractors, and a ruler (to do it well).

WHAT YOU NEED: You will need a wooden board. (Chip board will not work as well as plywood, and a regular wooden plank is best.) Check the scrap heap at a lumberyard. The board you use doesn't need to be square or even, though the design you make will be regular and symmetrical. You will need several spools of thread or string of different colors, a hammer, and a large quantity of brads or small nails. You will need black, white, or brightly colored paint for the board, and a brush to paint with. You'll also need paper for a pattern, a pencil, tape, and the compass, ruler, and protractor mentioned above.

DIRECTIONS: Paint the board completely, including the edges.

While the wood is drying, design a pattern. The easiest one to start with is a circle or a circle within a circle. The most important thing to remember is making string art is that you need an even or matching number of points. Mark the first point on the circle. (Remember that there are 360 degrees in a circle.) Use the protractor to make a dot every ten or twenty degrees. Choose one increment and use it for the entire circle. If you are making a circle within a circle, you can use the same spacing or change to a new spacing measurement for the second circle. Try five degrees for a very tight design.

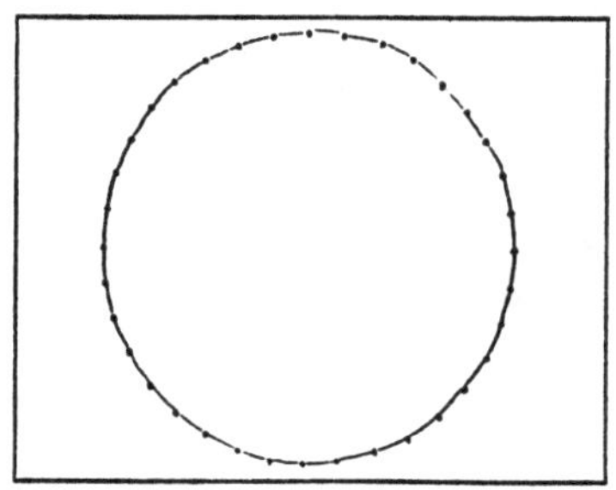

When the pattern is complete, tape it to the dry board. Hammer the brads or small nails through the paper at each of the point marks you made, and into the board to a depth of one half the nail length. Paint the nails the same color as the board and let them dry. Remove the pattern. Tie a thread to one nail. Count a number of nails to the right. Turn the thread around that nail. Count the same number of nails to the right and turn the thread around that nail. Go all around the circle one time. If you have used 18 or 20 nails, you may find that trying the thread every 5 or 6 nails works out well.

Now, tie a thread to the first nail and string it to the fifth nail. Next, string it to the tenth nail. Continue from the tenth nail to the fifteenth nail, and proceed as before. Alternate two to five colors completing the circle.

Experiment by changing the stringing procedure. On the inner circle, string from one nail to the one completely opposite. Return to the adjoining nail and complete the circle. Try stringing a closed circle, covering the whole area in one color, and then make a perimeter of colors using the first instructions.

To make a sail effect, draw an "L" shape on the pattern paper, using a ruler. Mark the same number of dots on the short horizontal line and the long vertical line. Space the dots evenly on the two lines. String the thread from the outside dot of one line to the inside dot of the other line. Carry the thread back and forth until the shape is complete. Try stringing from an outside dot to an outside dot for a different look.

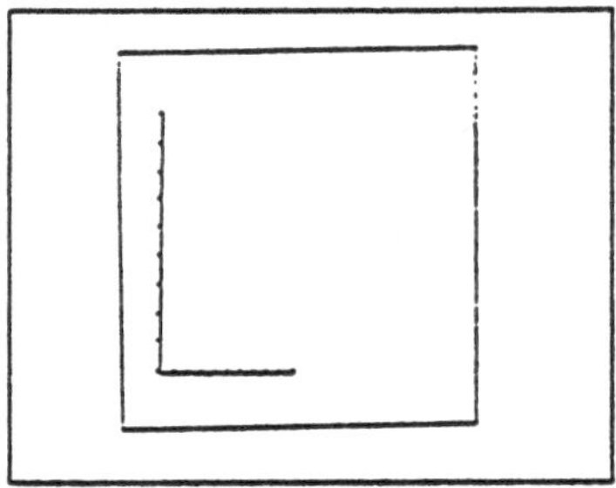

JUNK SCULPTURE

Junk sculpture is another activity for older children or teens. Junk can be glued with epoxy, or welded or soldered together. The way you decide to attach pieces together depends on your own workshop.

WHAT YOU NEED: You need a collection of miscellaneous metal discards. Wheels, gears, strips of fenders, cans, old tools, and other metal garbage make good sculptures. You also need tin snips.

DIRECTIONS: Start the sculpture with the largest and most stable piece of junk. Using a welding torch (and the proper safety-equipment), weld a second piece to the first. The pieces can also be epoxy-cemented or soldered together.

The construction is complete whenever you decide it is, or when you run out of junk. Leave it as is or spray-paint it. Mount the sculpture on a pedestal and add a 3 x 5 card with a grand title.

THING TREES

Even young children can make Thing Trees.

WHAT YOU NEED: You need a bare tree branch, a few small rocks or pebbles, and a chunk of clay or plaster of Paris. You'll need a large empty can--a coffee can is best. Get things to hang from the tree. Decorated, hollow Easter eggs are nice. You can also hang origami birds or straw butterflies, or even decorate the tree with paper loop chains.

DIRECTIONS: Stand the bare branch in the coffee can. Use a lump of clay to hold the branch and then fill the can with small rocks and pebbles. Instead of using clay, you can fill the can with pebbles and then pour the plaster of Paris in the can. Spray paint the can after the plaster dries, then hang the decorations on the branches.

The Display Nook

Now that you have had the opportunity to share such pleasurable times with your children, think of ways that you can preserve these memories.

Sharing memories helps tie your relationship closer and strengthen your family unit.

Develop a "Show-off" area in your home. Express pride in the children's achievements and in the things that you have done together. Give the children the opportunity to exhibit their endeavors, and to see how their abilities and capabilities have improved over a period of time.

If the children have their own room, you can hang all their pictures and put all their three-dimensional objects on shelves and dresser tops. When they complete something new (or bring something to your home that they made elsewhere), allow them to be displayed. If there is not much room, let your children decide which items to store and which to display. Keep a storage box marked with the year. Sometime in the future, you and your children will have a very enjoyable time reminiscing about the contents of those boxes.

If the apartment is not large enough to keep a constant display in view, try a temporary method. Mount the pictures and hanging crafts on the inside of a closet or pantry door where you can enjoy them every time the door is opened.

Another display area for hanging items can be made by attaching a square of cork to the reverse side of a framed picture hanging in your living room. When the children are visiting, reverse your pictures and pin their pictures to the cork, just as if it were a bulletin board.

For a large display area, which can be permanent or easily stored, build or buy a tri-fold screen. You might find one in a garage sale. Cover one side of the screen with paint or wallpaper that matches your walls and the other side with cork. Pin the children's displays to the cork. When you want a more formal look, just turn the screen around so that the plain side is exposed.

For a permanent display of non-hangable art work that can stay in your living room, purchase a plain, unpainted corner knick knack cabinet. Paint or stain it to match your walls or furniture. Help the children choose their best work to display.

You may be surprised at how much time you are actually spending with the children each weekend, and at the same time you may realize that in the past when your time together was endless, you didn't spend as much time together.

Enjoy your special times together, but be aware that there will still be difficult times. When those moments arise, share the memories you have collected with the children. Enjoy them again. Use them to pass over the rough times. Enjoy being sentimental. Believe it or not, your personal life and your lives together will become easier. Their childhood will pass quickly and you will have the pleasure of someday being able to look back at these times and remembering that being a weekend father was not too difficult.

BOOK TWO

Creating a New Home

BOOK TWO
CREATING A NEW HOME

Chapter 10

BOOK TWO

5

CREATING A NEW HOME

Starting a new life after a divorce is different than starting a new life in a marriage. No one is showering you with gifts, good wishes, and friendly advice. It is sad and a very lonely business, but it has to be done. The basic necessities must be taken care of first and then you can deal with more than just a daily existence.

First of all, you need a home and the things in a home that make it liveable. Although some newly divorced men start out with nothing, you hopefully were able to get some household items like furniture, kitchen cookware, and bed linens when you divided the contents of your house with your ex-wife. If not, you will need some basic furniture and goods, and you will find advice and suggestions on what to get, and where to get it, here.

It is very important to find a place to live that you feel you can call home. The day that you were separated from your family, your home, and your belongings, was very traumatic. The last thing on your mind was finding a special place to live. You might have moved in with a friend or relative, or rented a hotel or boarding house room. But now you must think about making a new life for yourself and you are really going to have to think about the place where you live. Think about where you are staying. Have you chosen a place in which you are happy? Can you bring your children here? Can you entertain? Can you relax when you come home from work?

If you are content, then no changes are necessary, but if you are not happy and you plan to make changes, keep the following suggestions in mind. First and foremost, take your personal needs and desires into consideration. You are the person who is going to live there all the time. Choose the kind of home that makes you feel most comfortable.

In all probability, the cost of housing will be uppermost in your mind, but there are other considerations as well. Make some basic decisions about location. Consider during the decision making process how easy it is to pick up the children, get to work, visit your folks, park your car, or get to public transportation. Check out the following establishments in the neighborhood: supermarkets, dry-cleaners, post office, drug stores, restaurants, bakeries, laundromats, delicatessens, churches or temples, and banks.

Make sure that it is a safe neighborhood. If your children are old enough to travel to your new home alone, is transportation close? Take a walking trip over the same streets that they will travel, then check the streets all around the area. Observe not only the adults in the area, but check the neighborhood for bullies and gangs. Be aware that an area that is safe for an adult is not necessarily safe for a child.

Find out if the landlord has any special rules. Can you have a pet? Can you have a water-bed? Can you get rid of garbage easily? Is there a bug problem? What are the neighbors like? Can you play your radio or stereo? How loud? And of course, can the children stay over?

Next, consider your transportation needs. What about parking your car? If you ride a motorcycle, will it be accepted? How about a pickup? Can you park on the street, or must your vehicle be in a driveway or parking lot?

If you use public transportation, can you travel to the supermarket by foot? Can you drag your portable marketing cart home easily? Do the local stores make deliveries? Do the restaurants have take-out service? Are the shops and services available at hours that are convenient for you?

If you are interested in athletics, are there playing fields, parks, and running tracks nearby? How do the neighborhood residents (and dogs) feel about joggers?

If possible, choose a home that gives you privacy. If you plan to have the children sleep over, consider a place with an extra room for the children, even if it does cost a little more. If it is not possible to get an extra room--and it can be as small as a hallway--try to choose one with extra space that you can arrange and have set up especially for the kids.

Make a choice that really pleases you; it will make your new life easier.

-+-

THE PLACE WHERE YOU LIVE

You can decorate your new home in a lavish manner or on a small budget. How much you spend is up to you. Examine your wallet and your resources and examine the type of life you plan, and then design a home that can meet those needs. Many newly divorced men are disappointed when they try to create a carbon copy of their old home. They should realize that it is impossible to do. Even if they could buy every matching piece of furniture and purchase a copy of all the pictures on their old walls they still cannot replicate their old home. Other men try to regain former lifestyles by purchasing the type of furnishings they would have had as young bachelors, while some don't decorate their homes at all, feeling that their lives are just too dismal to deal with aesthetics. Presuming that you don't want to live as austerely as a monk, and that you don't want to punish yourself by living in squalor, you will find some helpful information and hints here for making your new home comfortable.

While you are designing and decorating your new home, invite your children to help. Listen to their suggestions--they may have some very good ideas. Think about friends' homes you have visited and try to remember if there were styles or decorating ideas that always seemed pleasing to you. You can use the same ideas in your home. But, start inexpensively. You may have a very different idea about how you want to live in just a year or two.

If you have managed to get a place that has an extra room for the children, make sure that they share in the decorating of this space. If you are unable to get an apartment with an extra room, there are still some ways to help your children learn that your new home is their home, too. You will find suggestions throughout this book.

Your furniture needs can start out simply. You absolutely need a bed and a table and chairs immediately. When you are ready for more, you will find that there is a tremendous variety of furniture available and there are many kinds of furniture building plans, as well. You can borrow bits and pieces of furniture from friends and family, or buy furniture from newspaper personal "For Sale" ads or garage sales. If your future is still unsettled, rent your furniture by the piece or by the roomful. Check "Furniture-Rental" in the Yellow Pages. None of the choices you make now have to be permanent or expensive, but they should be comfortable.

Bedrooms and Sleeping Arrangements

The first thing to decide after renting your new home is where you sleep, and where your children sleep when they come over to visit.

Of course, families come in different sizes, and if you have five children you are going to have to do more planning than if you just have one. The ages of the children also make a difference.

Don't plan to have the child share your bed; neither of you will sleep well. For the first few visits bedrolls on the floor for you or the kids might be fun, but that kind of fun wears out pretty fast on a cold, hard floor. Try to keep any experience that leads to a backache, sleeplessness, or other discomforts to a minimum. If you are uncomfortable, the rest of the weekend will be miserable. You will find that settling sleeping arrangements early in the planning and decorating stages will most benefit you and the children.

A complete bedroom ideally contains a closet, a dresser, a night-table and, perhaps a chair. For your bedroom you will probably also need a phone, a clock, a radio, and a lamp. For the children's room, it would be nice to have a dresser, a chair, a play or work table, and hopefully a closet. Realistically, you can manage with less. But again, your comfort and pleasure will make your new life more bearable.

You can start furnishing your home with a purchased or borrowed dresser or even one that you have picked up at a garage sale. You can build cabinets or shelves or design a "high-tech" look using the new pipe and plastic furniture.

It is not a good idea to buy second-hand upholstered furniture because the fabric may be deeply soiled or even harbor bugs; on the other hand, painted or bruised wooden furniture can be sprayed for bugs, stripped, and re-finished.

A small wooden or metal two-drawer file makes an excellent night-table. If it locks, it can also be used to store legal documents and tax papers.

Discount, electronic, and telephone stores sell a combination radio-phone-lamp-clock that takes up a lot less room that the four individual items.

If your room lacks a closet, watch the office supply and rental ads for free-standing closets or clothes racks. You can also build or buy a clothes valet or clothes tree.

A dresser top covered with a quilted pad or carriage mattress makes an excellent changing table for a baby.

You will probably find that once your sleeping arrangements are complete, they will remain unchanged for a very long time. Spend the extra time and, if it is available, the extra money, to make you and the children as comfortable as possible.

BEDS AND MATTRESSES

Beds come in several sizes, shapes, styles, and designs. What is often called a standard bed varies a great deal. It may come with a headboard and footboard, or just a headboard, or with no headboard or footboard at all. You can purchase a metal frame to hold the spring and mattress, and purchase a headboard at a later date. You can even build a bed yourself.

First determine the amount of space available for a bed, and then consult the chart below for approximately sizes.

Bed and Fitted Sheet Size	Mattress	Flat Sheet	Blanket
Twin	39" X 75"	72" X 104"	66" X 90"
Double/Full	54" X 75"	81" X 104"	80" X 90"
Queen	60" X 80"	90" X 115"	90" X 90"
King	76" X 80"	108" X 115"	108" X 90"
Bunk/Cot	30" X 75"	30" X 75"	
Youth Bed	33" X 66"		
Crib	24" X 42"		Crib Size
	27" X 52"		Crib Size

You can get some very good ideas for decorating and coordinating the sleeping areas from the bedroom or sheet displays in department stores.

Use an extra sheet or pillowcase that matches your bedspread or sheet set, as a decorative device. For example, to make a mock headboard, mount a matching pillowcase on a wood or cardboard support with glue or staples, and then use an inexpensive picture frame to finish the project. Hang the completed "picture" on the wall over the head of the bed.

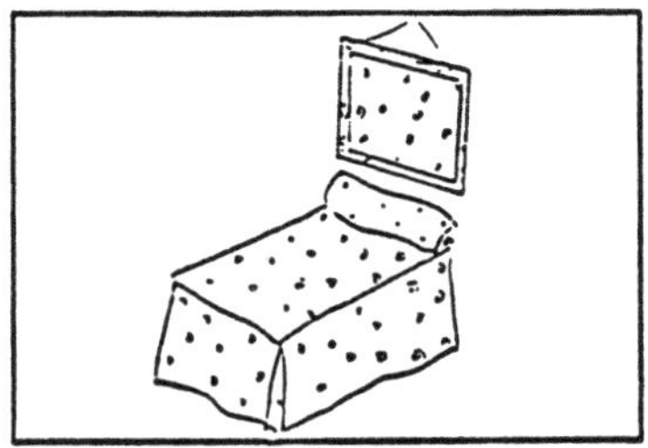

Another idea is to attach a curtain rod to the wall, quite high up, and hang a sheet from the rod by curtain hooks. That turns the entire wall into a headboard.

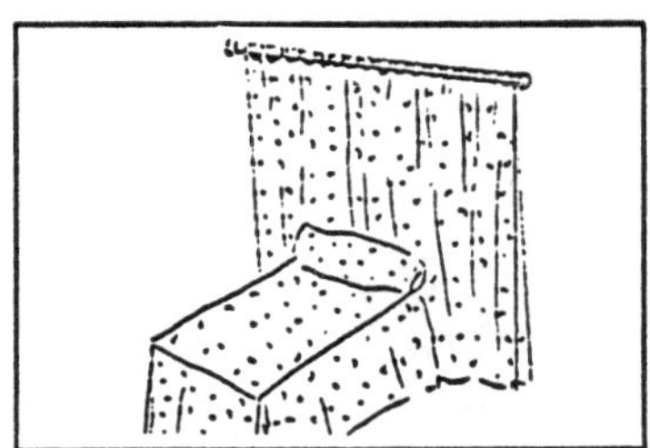

You can also make a simple headboard by stapling a sheet to a piece of plywood. Get a piece of plywood that is an inch wider than the width of the bed frame and one to two feet higher than the height of the frame plus mattress. Measure the board and purchase an extra flat twin sheet in the same pattern that you use on the bed. Sand and finish the plywood. Cover one side of the wood with the sheet, stapling it to the edges of the board. Trim the fabric back to the staples. Tack half-round molding over the join of the fabric and plywood edge to finish it. Stain or paint the trim before attaching it to the plywood. Drill holes through the base of the covered board and then bolt it to the bed frame.

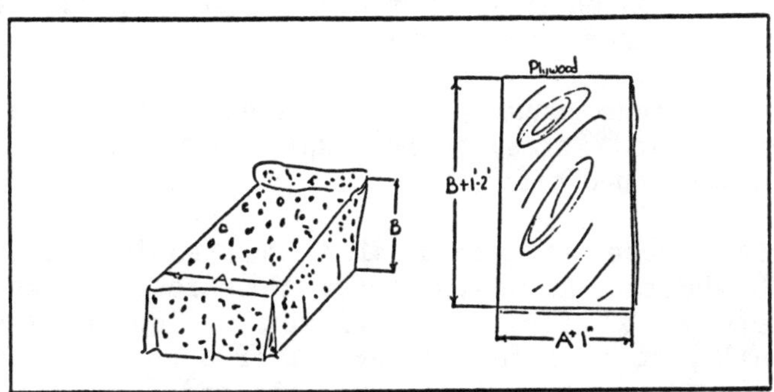

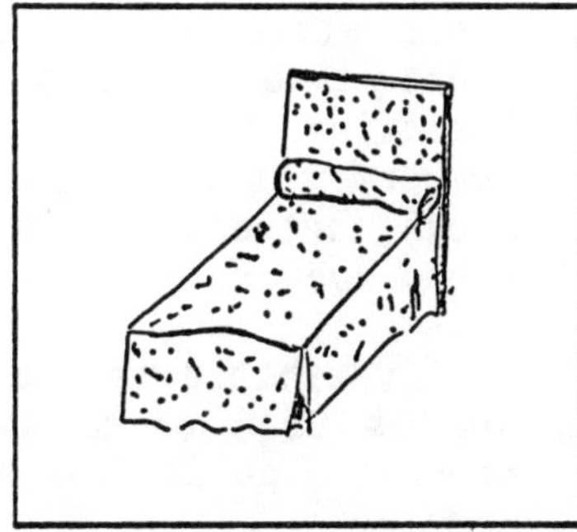

Mattresses and the support for a mattress (called an innerspring mattress) come in specific sizes and must fit the bed frame. Mattress sizes are youth (or bunk bed), twin, full, queen, king, and crib. The sizes for sheets use the same names.

If you want to use fitted or contour sheets (and that is highly recommended for saving bed-making time), you must use the correct match for the mattress size. Use a twin fitted sheet on a twin mattress, a queen fitted sheet on a queen size mattress, and so forth. If you use flat sheets, you have more leeway in the bed size because you can fold or tuck the sheets to fit, but for convenience do treat yourself to fitted sheets as soon as possible.

Water-beds usually require special sheets and blankets and it may be necessary to purchase them in a water-bed store.

Cribs are a special size and require fitted crib sheets, which are safer than folded larger sheets in a crib. Even if you do laundry frequently, be sure to get several crib sheets. You should also get at least two crib pads to protect the mattress from getting wet. You will probably find a friend or relative who has a crib stored in their attic. Since a child uses a crib for a short time, usually until three years of age, borrowing would be better than buying. Get bumpers for a crib so that the baby doesn't get caught between the bars or bump his head if he is a bed rocker.

A youth bed mattress is smaller than twin size and is used on a bed with side protectors that prevent a child from rolling out.

You can purchase protector bars in some furniture or medical supply stores and attach them to any bed. You can also back heavy chairs up to the bed to create a barrier as a temporary safety measure. A youth bed is meant for one child up to 6-8 years. After the child reaches that age, you can remove the side bars, and use the bed as a twin bed. Bunk beds come in a special size and also in twin size. A twin size mattress is meant for one child or adult.

A full size mattress (also known as a double size) can be used by two slim adults who sleep quietly. For more sleeping room, choose a queen or king size bed.

Mattresses come in different degrees of firmness and often have names that sound as if they cure back ailments. Disregard the names. There is only one way to tell how a mattress feels--by sleeping on it for a month. Since that is not possible, lie down on it in the store. Most people feel too shy to test a bed in public, but it is worth the few minutes of embarrassment to avoid years of discomfort. Take your shoes off and climb completely on the bed. Wiggle around. Feel if buttons or decorative stitching annoy you. Make sure that the support bar in a convertible sofa doesn't press across your back, or you will end up feeling crippled.

Pressing a mattress with your hands is like kicking a tire to check out a car. You might find out something, but it won't be important. Various mattresses with similar descriptions or names feel different when you lie on them. Take the time to personally lie on them and compare so that you can make a more educated decision. Try not to let the cost influence you to purchase an inferior product.

Be concerned with the filling contents of the mattress. Some mattresses are filled with animal hair and some with natural fibers, while others are filled with grasses, man-made fibers, or combinations of fibers and hair. Be sure that the mattresses you buy won't set off someone's allergies.

Rotate your mattresses just like your tires. Turn it over left to right, making the bottom the top, every six months. Turn it head to foot, without turning it over, every three months.

PILLOWS

Pillows also come in several sizes, the two most popular being standard and king. Unless you absolutely must have a very long pillow (king), get the standard size. Standards are much easier to find, and to store, are less expensive, and come in more choices of firmness and filling content. It is also easier to get pillow cases for standard size pillows. Keep in mind that if you have unexpected company, you can always use throw pillows for sleeping-pillows, or you can stuff your extra sleeping-pillows into fancy covers and use them for decorative or scatter pillows. In general, remember than when you have limited space or limited finances, it is always helpful to use furniture, decorations, or accessories in several ways.

SHEETS AND PILLOW CASES

You will find that the cost of bed linen (sheets, spreads, comforters) gets increasingly expensive as the size gets larger. It is possible though to get sheets at reasonable prices at a "White Sale." Department stores have "White Sales" several times a year. Most stores advertise at least one sheet design that is specially priced to attract customers to the store. You can also find special prices during inventory clearances or when a pattern is discontinued. It is possible to find sheets with patterns and weaves similar to the more expensive styles at discount stores.

Sheets are usually purchased in sets consisting of a fitted bottom sheet and a flat top sheet. If it is a twin set, it includes one case. If the set is marked full, queen or king, it contains two cases. If you don't need a complete set, it is usually possible to buy one sheet or a separate package of pillow-cases.

Sheets have different weaves, and the weave, as well as the dimensions, determine the price. The coarsest weave is called muslin. Look at the printed description on the package. If the number of stitches per square inch ranges between 112 and 140, the sheets will be coarser, less expensive, and will probably last longer. However, the coarser sheets will not be as comfortable as percale. Percale sheets are softer, finer, and lighter, and have 180 or more stitches per inch.

Definitely buy sheets that don't need ironing!

If you don't like to sleep on cold sheets in the winter, buy flannel sheets. If you can't find flannel sheets in a local store, you can order them from a camping supply catalog. You can even use a flat flannel sheet as a summer blanket.

BLANKETS

When you buy blankets, check for their fiber content and cleaning instructions. If you like to roll up in your blanket, get one larger than the size of your bed. Electric blankets should be the same size as the size of your mattress--twin blanket for twin bed and so forth. Electric blankets are light weight and maintain a pleasant temperature. If the heat in your apartment is turned down at night and you like to sleep in warmth, they are very comfortable. Check the washing instructions; most electric blankets can be machine washed and dried. Don't get an electric blanket for a young child or a bed-wetter. Get small blankets for youth beds and cots and crib blankets for cribs. Don't take a chance on a child getting caught or smothered by an oversized blanket.

MATTRESS PADS

Mattress pads come in the same sizes as fitted sheets and mattresses. Mattress pads for adult beds are quilted and crib pads are rubberized. The mattress pad is an expensive item but by covering a mattress you can protect it from dust, dirt, stains, moisture, and anything else you don't particularly want as a permanent mark. It's a good barrier for coffee, pets, kiddies, and wet towels. Although sheets should be laundered once a week, the mattress pad on an adult's bed can be washed every couple of months, unless wet or soiled. Launder children's mattress pads more frequently, and wash crib pads after each weekend visit or when they get wet.

MORE ABOUT BEDS

Although mattresses and sheets are standardized, bed styles are not. You can find a bed or beds to fit any spatial need or personal preference. You can buy a bed with a metal or a wood frame, or with no frame at all. Some beds rest on a support structure that looks like a box. These platforms can be very simple or ornate and upholstered. Water-beds are supported by a special type of platform.

If you lack space, you can buy cots that fold up and store in small places. If you enjoy camping think about the dual use of camping cots. Cots come in narrow, twin, and full size, and they can be rented. You can find cots with springs and a separate mattress or cots with canvas suspended between support bars.

At one time the Murphy Bed(c) was the only convertible furniture. The Murphy Bed was a folded bed which sprang from its hiding place in a specially built closet hung on a wall. Recently, this kind of bed has returned to popularity, but now it folds into a cabinet-like piece of furniture.

Another folding bed is the futon. The futon is a Japanese styled mattress bed which unfolds flat on the floor for sleeping. It gets refolded into a chair or couch form, and buckles, clips, or velcro straps keep it closed in that position.

Sleeping couches or sofas, often called convertibles, come in sizes from full to king. When closed they can be used in the living room or family room as a loveseat or couch. There are even living room styled upholstered chairs and hassocks that open into single beds.

Other beds that have dual use are the daybed or Hollywood bed. When you are ready to go to bed you remove the cover and the throw pillows, or those long cylindrical or triangular back pillows called bolsters, and it changes from sitting furniture to sleeping furniture. The trundle bed also converts from one use to another, but has in addition a second mattress and spring hidden under the top mattress, spring and frame. The trundle opens into two twin beds.

An innovation in sleeping arrangements and styled on the bunk-bed concept (one bed above the other), is the single bed supported by a dresser. Bunk-beds can also be arranged at right angles to each other, incorporating dressers, desks, ladders, storage and play areas.

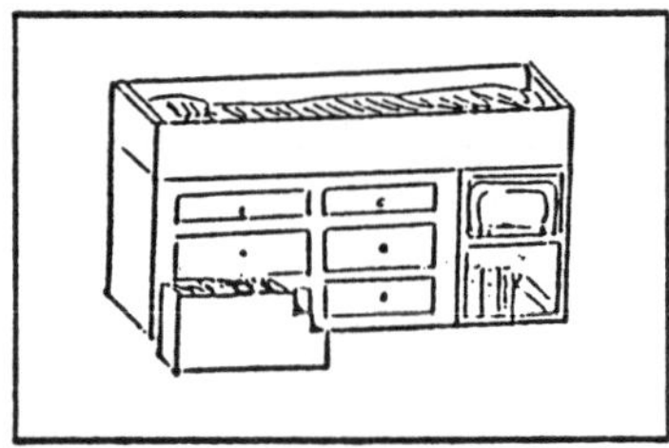

Another idea for small areas is the Captain's Bed. Based upon the space-conserving ideas used on a ship, this bed is built on a platform that includes dresser drawers in its base. These and other built-ins utilize small spaces efficiently.

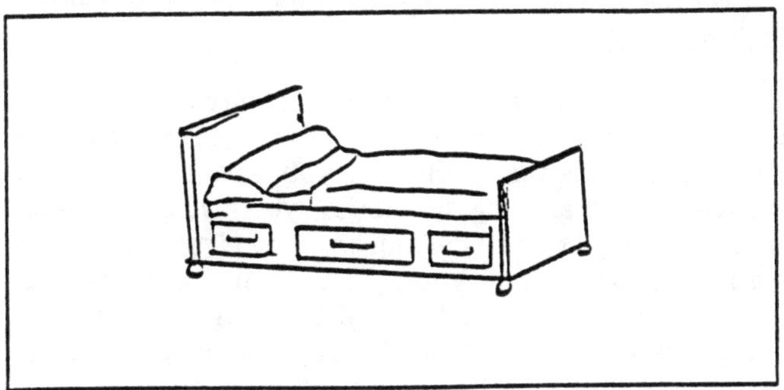

WATER BEDS

Water beds come with some special considerations, weight being the primary one. A cubic foot of water weights almost 63 pounds. If you plan to live in a basement apartment or in a one-story house with a substantial slab foundation, there will probably be no weight problem. Anywhere else, there might be. If you are planning to buy your first waterbed, spend a few nights sleeping on a friend's waterbed first. Make sure that a water source is easily accessible. More important, make sure that you can empty it easily. Arrange for leak insurance if you have someone living below you. Let the children know immediately if they can play on the waterbed.

Eating Arrangements

The second most important decision you have to make in your new home concerns your eating arrangements.

If you grab juice and coffee on your way to work, have lunch at your desk and stop at a restaurant for dinner, your kitchen is not going to seem important. But if you plan to cook meals for your children and eat at home, some planning should be done.

It is necessary to again evaluate your budget and living style in order to design the best eating arrangements. Unless you are a superb cook and love entertaining at home, you will not need a formal dining room. Plan an eating area large enough for you and your children, and possibly guests, to sit in, and bright enough to read the morning paper. If the living room has a nice view, place your table so that you can enjoy the view. It's not always necessary to eat in the kitchen.

TABLES, CHAIRS, AND EATING AREAS

Some homes have dining rooms, some eating areas, some eat-in kitchens, and some eating islands. The eating island is a counter, usually adjacent to a food preparation area. Most islands are fairly high and require a stool rather than a chair. Although at first the island might seem fun, a child may find it much more awkward than a conventional table and chair. A kitchen with an area large enough for table and chairs is the easiest to keep clean.

Examine how your new home is arranged. It is possible to use rooms differently from the way they are defined. For instance, a dining area attached to a living room could be used for a mini-bedroom, while the entrance hallway substitutes as the eating area. It's also possible to use a room or part of a room in several different ways. Just as a convertible sofa is a couch by day and a bed by night, convertible tables (with sides that fold down), can be used for end-tables during the day and dining tables for meals at night. There are round coffee tables that rise to the height of a dining table, with a screw action like an old fashioned piano stool.

The most familiar in hideaways are the folding card table and chairs. These can slip into the closet when not being used.

The top of a gateleg table is divided into a narrow top and two very long leaves that fold down to the floor. A 70" long table can take up only 10" of space. There are gateleg tables that hide their matching chairs inside the space created by the two folded leaves.

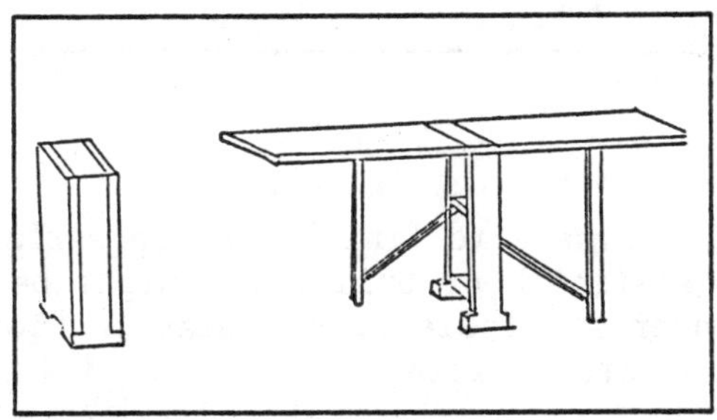

You can create a table that can be easily stored and can have a number of uses including dining table, work area, play area, and craft or carpentry area, by simply using a hollow core door or piece of plywood on saw horses. If you make the saw horses yourself, remember that the height of a regular table is 30-31".

Keep the thickness of the door in mind when cutting the saw horse legs.

You can also create a folding shelf table. Using strong hinges, attach a shelf made from 1" plywood to the wall, so that it folds up. Use strong rope or lightweight chain to help support the shelf in its extended perpendicular position. If it has to bear a great deal of weight, add a support leg.

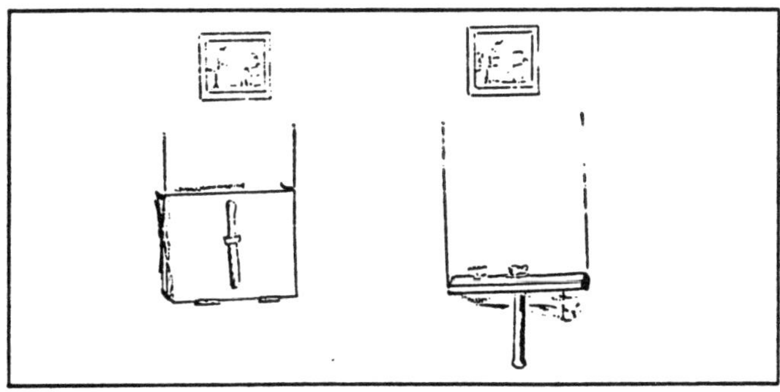

Use polyurethane to finish the top surface of a table you re-finish or build. It might be a good idea to cover any table with a plastic cloth when the children are visiting.

You can get kitchen or dining room furniture in department, discount and specialty stores. There are also special outlets and warehouses for all the large department stores where you can usually find slightly blemished or over stocked selections. These stores, often nick-named "Scratch and Dent," have a varied selection at good prices, but examine the furniture well. Of course, there are tag sales and garage sales.

Try garage sales for highchairs. Like cribs, their use-life is short. When you look for a highchair, try to find one that converts to a student's chair (i.e., one that can be pulled up to the table without the tray), or that can have other uses. A car seat carefully attached to a kitchen chair can serve as a baby's chair.

You can use a piece of furniture in unusual ways and then later on use it in the traditional way. For instance, a picnic table and benches can be used indoors until you are ready to buy regular dinette furniture. Then it could be moved to the children's room for a play table, or outside to a patio, terrace, or yard to be used in the conventional manner. If your kitchen is large but lacks cabinets, purchase two 30" high (heights must match) cabinets and place them side by side or back to back. Use them for a table base, adding a one-half inch board, table top size.

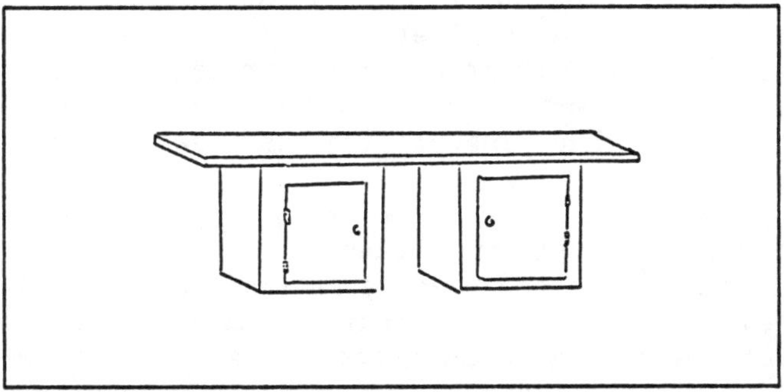

TABLE SETTINGS

A table looks more cheerful if you have placemats or a tablecloth on it. There are packages of paper placemats available in the supermarkets. Use one once and toss it out. Use throw-aways like paper towels, paper napkins, or paper placemats for convenience. Use washable fabric dish towels, rags, napkins, and so on for economy.

When you first start out, buy paper or foam dishes. They come in all sizes and shapes, including bowls, divided platters, dinner plates, and bread plates. They are attractive enough to look like china, and you don't have to wash them.

When you are ready for regular dishes, consider getting a set of stoneware dishes. They are attractive, inexpensive, and most are dishwasher-safe. Before buying any dishes turn one of the plates over. The back is marked with information about where they were made, and whether they are dishwasher- or microwave-safe.

Stoneware is often conventional-oven safe as well. Plastic dishes can also be attractive and inexpensive, but cannot be used in as many ways as stoneware.

Before putting any dishes or food in cabinets, make sure that the cabinets are clean. Sprinkle a trail of boric acid around all four edges of every cabinet shelf and drawer. Boric acid is a great deal safer than insecticide and gets rid of roaches.

A complete set of dishes usually contains 4 sets of 5 pieces (20 pieces) and includes 4 dinner plates, 4 salad or bread/butter plates, 4 cereal (soup) bowls, and 4 cups and saucers. Sometimes the set also includes a serving platter, a serving bowl, a sugar container and a cream/gravy container. Be sure that the children can use the dishes you buy--don't purchase anything so fragile that they can't use them.

Silverware (most people use stainless steel) also comes in sets of 20 pieces, containing 4 knives, 4 forks, 4 salad/dessert forks, 4 teaspoons, and 4 cereal/soup spoons. These sets also may come with serving pieces. Before making your purchase, take the stainless out of its package and handle it as though you were going to eat with it. Make sure that the handle pattern or edge doesn't dig into your hand. See that it is utilitarian and not fragile. You will probably need to add a set of steak knives, a paring knife, and a carving knife to your shopping list.

Although paper, plastic, or foam cups are great for everyday use, you may want to get glasses eventually. The most necessary are juice glasses, water or milk glasses, and possibly wine or highball glasses. If you enjoy beer, you might want to add beer mugs or steins.

KITCHEN COOKWARE AND GADGETS

It is not necessary to buy every gadget or appliance immediately.

Keep a pad and pencil in the kitchen and make a note of the items that you reach for, but lack. If you look for a specific gadget twice, you probably need it.

To start out, for simple cooking, get one large and one small frying pan and a few pots. You need a coffee pot or tea kettle, a pot large enough for cooking spaghetti or corn, and two smaller pots. One of the smaller pots should be a quart size and the other should hold a pint.

You may want a toaster or a toaster oven, but you can make toast in the oven for a while.

To complete your basic kitchen, you'll need a drainer to dry the dishes (if you don't have a dishwasher), and two pot holders to protect your hands. Add salt shakers, a butter dish, a can opener, and a can punch. (The last item used to be called a beer can opener before the tab became popular, but is still used for juice.) You also need a colander/strainer, measuring cups and spoons, a pancake turner/spatula, a long handled fork, and a slotted spoon. The spoon can lift everything out of a pot from cooked vegetables to boiled eggs. There are wall rack sets that include the long handled fork, slotted spoon, pancake turner, and other items. It may be more convenient to get the whole set. If you enjoy wine, don't forget a corkscrew.

Many gadgets have more than one use. For instance, you can use ice-tongs for salad tongs or spaghetti tongs. Kitchen shears are handy for cutting coupons, plastic freezer packages, or chicken wings. A kitchen timer is very handy, and can be used for timing in your dark-room, timing a sun-tan, or as a reminder alarm.

MICROWAVE OVENS

If your budget allows a large purchase at this time, treat yourself to a microwave oven. Since it takes so little time to turn a frozen meal into a quick supper, you will find that it is easy to eat supper at home. The microwave is also cool, easy to clean, and fairly economical to use. You can cook a large meal like lasagna or a roast in the microwave with no loss of taste or moisture. Even warmed-over spaghetti tastes good. And potatoes bake in the time it takes you to wash up for dinner. If you need extra persuasion, check out this math: if you buy a simple microwave for approximately $200 and warm 100 commercial frozen food dinners averaging $4.00 each, you will have spent the same as 72 restaurant meals at approximately $7.50 plus tip. When you have eaten those 100 microwave meals (20 work weeks of 5 days each, or 14 weeks), you still have the microwave.

A microwave is great for warming a baby bottle, too.

Frozen meals (they used to be called T.V. dinners, but that name is inadequate now) come in all sizes, diets, and ethnic diversity. You can find Chinese food, Mexican food, kosher food, diet plates, haute cuisine, fish, fowl, vegetables and vegetarian platters, and so on. Check the directions for cooking. Some come on microwaveable plates, while others must stay inside their cardboard box or be transferred to a heatable plate.

STOCKING A PANTRY

When you initially stock your pantry and fill the refrigerator with basics, you are going to spend a fair portion of your budget, but you need not repurchase most of the basic stock for quite a while. Refilling used-up items doesn't ever cost as much as the initial stocking because they never are all finished at the same time. Creating a basic pantry makes it possible to have meals that are interesting, and to be ready for guests or entertaining. It also saves going out in the rain or snow for a basic ingredient when you are cooking. The following list should be used as a suggestion only.

SEASONINGS: salt, pepper, garlic, dry onion, paprika, oregano, basil, cinnamon, vanilla extract

COOKING AND SALAD OIL: corn oil, olive oil, hydrogenated fat (Crisco(R))

CONDIMENTS: mayonnaise, mustard, ketchup, relish, pickles, Worcestershire sauce, tomato sauce, steak sauce, grated cheese

SOUPS AND GRAVIES: assorted canned or packaged soups, assorted canned or packaged gravy mixes

PASTA: spaghetti, macaroni, noodles, and rice

MEAT AND FISH: canned tuna, sardines or salmon, canned luncheon meats, chili, Vienna sausages, chicken, macaroni or ravioli with meat

CEREALS: breakfast cereals for children and for yourself

BEVERAGES: instant or brewable coffee, tea, iced tea mix, fruit juice, packaged fruit drinks (Kool Aid(R) or Tang(C)), cocoa, baby formula, soda, mixers

SNACKS: cookies, crackers, peanut butter, jelly, cheese spread, chips

VEGETABLES: assorted cans of peas, stringbeans, potatoes, sweet potatoes or yams, carrots, beans, beets, asparagus, and so on. Instant potato flakes

DESSERTS: fruit, puddings, cake mix, raisins, nuts

DRY FOODS: flour, pancake-flour, sugar, powdered milk, bread crumbs

FROZEN FOODS: vegetables, fried potatoes, waffles, prepared meals, pizza

FRESH FRUIT AND VEGETABLES: salad vegetables, onions, potatoes, fruit

FRESH MEAT, FISH OR FOWL

EGGS, BUTTER, MILK, AND BREAD

If you live in an area where it is warm or humid, put pasta, cereal and flour products in the freezer for 24 hours to kill any insect larvae. Then put those foods in sealed glass jars or plastic containers.

You might want to purchase at the same time you are stocking your pantry, the following cleaning supplies: broom, dust pan, carpet sweeper or vacuum, mop, detergent for washing floors, cleanser for bathroom, scouring pads, dish detergent, laundry detergent, and furniture polish.

Be careful where you store cleaning supplies. Most of them are poisonous or caustic.

KIDS IN THE KITCHEN

When you are in a hurry, your children don't belong in the kitchen. Accidents happen easily when people get in the way. But when you have time, or can make time, even young children enjoy participating in kitchen chores that you can do together. Washing and drying dishes is a good time to talk. Older children can cook, using almost any appliance after they have been taught how. Young children can stir or mix ingredients prior to cooking. Allowing the children in the kitchen makes your home their home, too.

The Rest of the House

The bedroom and kitchen have priority in your planning, because as is obvious, you have to eat and sleep as soon as you move into your new home, but you also need to wash and use the bathroom.

The major purchase for the bathroom is towels. Buy enough towels to allow you to go two weeks without doing laundry, even if you plan to do laundry every week. Then add a few more for the children. Compare the sizes of bath towels. The name "bath" implies a large towel but they vary so much that some should be re-named. Hand towels are the small towel used for decorative purposes more than anything else. If your budget is small, just get bath towels and wash cloths. Get several more of the handy wash cloths than you think you need for the bathroom. You can use them for bibs, toss a damp cloth in a plastic bag for traveling, or leave another damp one (in a plastic bag) in the freezer for an emergency ice pack.

Purchase a toothbrush for each child that can be left in your bathroom. Keeping things that the children recognize as theirs helps them get used to your new home. If they have a favorite toothpaste, get that, too. Use paper cups or plastic glasses in the bathroom. It's cleaner, more sanitary, and safer than glass.

If your bathroom doesn't have a hamper, use a large laundry basket lined with a plastic garbage bag. Keep detergent and powdered bleach in a small plastic bag right in the basket and it is always ready for the laundromat.

Get a shower-curtain and a liner if the tub doesn't have a glass enclosure. Buy only the liner if your budget won't allow both. It won't be necessary to get a bathmat at first. Use one of the towels on the floor and then place it on the tub edge to dry.

Check the bath tub for safety. Use bath tub friction tape (it comes in strips or flowers) on the bottom, and check bath tub water temperature when children use the tub.

Once the three most important living areas are ready, you can take a little more time for decorating any other living areas. As a matter of fact, use some extra time on purpose, to examine what you have accomplished and where you are going.

6

RULES FOR LIVING

Every home must work under some kind of direction and set of rules. Even the most informal living arrangement needs a framework within which all participants can live together. Some rules are necessary for maintaining good relations with a landlord, the neighbors, or the community at large. Some are guidelines to promote good health and good health habits. Some of the rules are designed to create a feeling of privacy, while others help allay fears and prevent problems. And, some rules are just good common sense.

Landlord—Imposed Rules

Landlords have contractual rules built into leases. For instance, your lease might state that your rent must be paid by mail, to be received by the first of the month by a rental agent. There are usually set rules and conditions for such matters as removal of garbage, use of garbage chutes and dumpsters, elevator courtesy, parking, and permanent guests. You probably have to contact an agent or superintendent to order repairs, and you may not be allowed to hammer nails in the walls. Frequently, there are rules about pool privileges, waterbeds, use of the laundry room, mail, quiet hours, and so on.

Most landlords do not mind weekend or vacation

visits by children. However, in some housing labeled "Adult Living," stay-over visits may be limited. Check these rules and make sure that your children understand them. Do not allow the children to become nuisances to your new neighbors.

In a private home rental, apartment sublet, or the rental of part of a private home, you are still involved in a landlord-tenant relationship. Be aware of all restrictions before you move in.

Health Rules

The basic rules for good health apply wherever you live. Don't allow your sensible eating or sleeping habits to change just because of your change in marital status. Become aware of those health rules that can particularly affect your children.

Although it often seems impossible to break an old habit, changes can be made. Once good habits and routines are established, they are easy to maintain.

Because you are now living in a new environment, and have made other changes in your life, learn new (good) habits to replace old ones. Help the children to do the same. For instance, it's very hard to break a habit like nail biting--your nails are always with you. So, learn a new habit. When you start to put your finger in your mouth, stop and count to 15. That's all. When you really become aware of the fact that you are getting ready to chew, add another trick to the pattern--press your hands together and count to 15 again. By learning the intermediate habit of recognizing the times when you are about to chew your nails, you learn the control you need to learn the ultimate, new habit of not biting your nails. You can use this type of behavior modification to stop smoking or lose weight, too.

HEALTH RECORDS AND HEALTH CARE

If you have moved to a new neighborhood and therefore plan to change your doctor or dentist, get recommendations from your old doctors and your new neighbors. Make medical arrangements before you need them.

Take time to check out the hospital nearest to your new home. See their emergency room. Find out how to contact the hospital and other emergency services. Many ambulance services are run by independent companies. Find out whether you call for an ambulance directly or go through the police or fire department to make the call. Check your medical insurance for coverage. Check for hospital satellite centers and medical service centers. They are often available for emergencies when your own doctor is not.

Get a list of all the immunizations that the children have had, and with their help keep it up to date. Make sure that you also have a list of all their allergies and special needs. If the children use any prescription drugs, ask their doctor for a duplicate prescription to keep at your home. Be sure that you know how to administer the drugs, how frequently they are given, and in what manner.

Learn to recognize the signs and symptoms of common illnesses. Children frequently exhibit very definite changes in their skin and appearance when they are sick or coming down with something. Look for a glazed expression or unusually bright eyes. Those changes, or bright pink patches on their cheeks may indicate a fever. Watch out for a pallor or cold sweat. A child who is getting sick might feel very tired and probably will be disinterested in what is going on. Many childhood illnesses start with rashes. Use calamine to soothe the itching.

Get a copy of a good child-care book that explains how to recognize and care for illness and keep it handy. Remember to take it with you on trips.

When a child is ill or seems to be getting ill, have him lie down and stay quiet. Don't let the child get chilled. In order to help the sick child not feel left out or ostracized, include the child in the activities you are doing with your other children through your conversation. Children don't know how to control their own illness--you have to do it for them.

SAFETY

Have a clearly-printed emergency list that the children can easily read posted next to each phone. The list should include numbers for the police, fire department, poison control center, hospital or other emergency center, the doctor, your work number, and their mother's home and work numbers. Also, include the telephone numbers of two neighbors that you feel are competent to deal with emergencies, and to whom you have introduced your children. Remember that you might have an accident, and have to send a child for help.

Children react in different ways to divorce. Some become nervous and tense, while others don't seem to be visibly affected. Some children try to manipulate their parents by threatening to run away; others do run away. Your divorce is stressful and threatening to them. Be prepared for unusual situations, responses, and emergencies.

Have an up-to-date photograph of each child. If service organizations are having fingerprinting or video-taping sessions in your area, take advantage of the opportunity for child identification. If your children travel by bus, train, or plane to visit you, ask their mother to plan ahead as to what they will wear while traveling. Ask her to take a picture of the children wearing those outfits, and make two copies of the pictures. Have her keep one copy and mail the other to you a couple of weeks before the children leave for their visit. When the children return to their mother, have them wear the same outfits. Have both parents' names and phone numbers pinned inside the children's clothes, or written with waterproof marker or ink in a blank press-on name tag.

Warn the children about unsavory individuals and unsafe conditions in your new neighborhood. Remind them of the safety rules they have learned in the past. Acquaint and educate them about unfamiliar but potentially dangerous hazards like dumpsters and old refrigerators. The change in your living style probably means a change in their normal environment, and they have to become aware of new threats.

Make up a first aid kit. Include children's aspirin or aspirin substitute, band-aids, gauze pads, a small scissor, a disposable wash cloth, antiseptic cream and spray, a mild laxative and Kaopectate(c) or something else to stop diarrhea. Include Ipecac(c) to induce vomiting in case of ingestion of poisons. Include tweezers, cotton, hydrogen peroxide, alcohol, calamine lotion and an antihistamine. Keep a child's thermometer and know how to use it. Drugstores sell a thermal strip for determining if a child has a fever, which is simpler to use than a thermometer but does not indicate the actual temperature. Keep a small box of sanitary napkins or tampons for a teen-aged daughter. It might be a good idea to get a heating pad, too.

Ask your doctor or pharmacist for suggestions for other first-aid items. Once the first-aid box is prepared, keep it in a place the children cannot reach unless they are old enough to trust with the contents.

All drugs, pills, medicines, vitamins, toiletries, as well as all cleaning materials like soap, chlorine bleach, ammonia, oven cleaner, bathroom and toilet cleaners, and detergent should be where children can not get into them. The same thing applies to all substances containing harmful chemicals like paints, paint thinners, hobbyist's glue, bug killers, plumbing de-cloggers, and photography chemicals (be extra careful of those that need to be stored in the refrigerator.)

Very often there are duplicates of these items in the kitchen, bathroom, workshop, and garage. Make sure that all potentially dangerous substances are out of the reach of young children.

Remember--household chemicals can maim or kill.

GOOD NUTRITION

It is really not difficult (and a lot less expensive) to eat nourishing meals at home instead of eating out all the time. Most children like simple, recognizable food. Hamburgers, chicken, and hot dogs don't bore them. See the "Cooking Book" section for some fun food suggestions.

Good nutrition dictates that adults and children eat portions from each of the five "Food Groups" every day. The following suggested diet regimen can be altered if you are a vegetarian, but make sure that your diet is nutritionally balanced and meets all the needs of a growing child. Teenagers need larger portions than small children or most adults.

DAIRY GROUP

(Milk, Cheese, Ice Cream)

- 1 quart daily for a child
- 1 pint daily for an adult

- 2 tablespoons butter or margarine

EGGS

- 4-5 a week for a child
- 2-3 a week for an adult
  possibly a few extra a week for cooking

VEGETABLES AND FRUITS

- 4-5 servings daily
- plus 1 serving daily of citrus fruit or tomatoes
- 1 serving daily of potatoes
- 1 serving daily of leafy green or yellow vegetables
- plus 1 fruit
  Include several servings per week of vegetables in the cabbage family like Broccoli

PROTEIN

(Meat, fish, poultry, or dried peas/beans)
. 1 portion daily

BREADS AND CEREALS

(Bread, cereal, pasta, rice)
. 3-4 portions daily, preferably whole grain

When you take your children out to eat, take them to places that fit their age. Most fast-food restaurants cater to children and serve the kind of food that they enjoy. Children don't have the sophisticated taste for spices and flavorings that adults have. Experiment and save the trip to a new restaurant for an adult companion. Then, if the menu is acceptable and the atmosphere is right, take the children on a later trip.

Plan meals for specific times, even if you are on a trip or away from home. Hungry children get cranky and crabby. Make sure when you are traveling that the children get enough fluids and enough bathroom stops to be comfortable. Don't forget to carry any prescribed medicines.

SLEEPING HABITS

It is important to maintain good sleep habits. Tired children get grumpy and tired adults are even worse. Do all the chores associated with setting up the sleeping arrangements when the children are not too tired and sleepy to help. Lay out their pajamas and other sleeping needs before their actual bedtime. Invite them to keep a favorite sleeping toy in your house.

Never make going to bed a threat. Bed time should be as pleasant as possible--don't save the evenings with your children to rehash all of the day's problems or incidences of misbehavior. Instead, save this time to review the good things that you did together, and for making plans for the next day or weekend.

FIRE DRILLS

It is extremely important to develop emergency plans and have fire drill practice. Your children must be very well trained on how to leave your home in an emergency. Teach them how to open locked doors and show them alternate ways to exit your apartment or home.

Visit your local fire department with the children and request a "Learn Not To Burn" kit. Teach the children how to crawl across the floor of a smoke-filled apartment, and how to check for fire in hallways or other rooms by feeling the door. Determine an emergency meeting place in and outside your home. Teach your children that in case of fire they must get out of the house and to the meeting place. Explain that they are not to return to the house to retrieve anything, including brothers and sisters.

Sometimes, well-meaning neighbors insist on taking a child in with them. Don't try to return to the scene of a fire to look for a missing child. Let the professional fire fighters know, and then check at neighbors for a missing child.

Rules in General

The following is a guide and list of suggestions where some kind of rule might apply. Because people's lives and needs vary so greatly, you will have to decide if an area is relevant or not.

Knowing ahead of time that there are areas, situations, or topics that are sensitive or potential problems makes it easier to deal with. Clear and precise rules, declared when you are not upset, are easier to follow.

RULES ABOUT SOUND

Discuss and decide with the children whether everyone can turn on the radio, stereo or T.V. Discuss volume level. If you plan to control the type of programming children may watch, let them know ahead of time.

Make decisions about practicing musical instruments. Determine if there is an apartment-house sound curfew. Many apartments request no noise after 10:00 or 11:00 P.M.

Discuss how noisily they may play. Make decisions about floor toys (like trucks or blocks) and floor games.

Find out whether it's necessary to wear slippersocks on bare floors and how the neighbors feel about children playing in the halls, gardens, or party rooms of the apartment.

Find out if noise restrictions include the sounds of late night toilet flushing.

RULES FOR SHARING

Determine ahead of time how things are to be shared. Do the oldest child and the youngest get the same sized portions? Who goes first? What are the car seating arrangements? In a new or unexpected situation, how will the rules apply? Who decides how, where, or when?

BATHROOM RULES

When making bathroom rules, consider the number of bathrooms and the number and sexes of your children. Use your rules to determine how and when the bathroom should be cleaned, and who does it.

Decide on the priority of use of the bathroom. (Probably that decision will have to be based on who has the best bladder control.) How do you feel about toilet seats left up or down? If you have a pet, does it like to get drinks from the toilet? Now, how do you feel about leaving the seat up or down? Is there a toilet paper brand preference? Does it matter which way it unrolls from the holder? How does your daughter dispose of sanitary napkins? Do the kids clean the bathroom?

How about hair in the sink? Do you need a rule about capping or squeezing the toothpaste? How do you store toothbrushes? Does your shower curtain go in or out of the tub? What do you do with wet towels or a wet bath mat?

When thinking about bathroom rules, think about who should empty the bathroom wastebasket? How often? How will you handle phone calls when you are in the bathroom, and may a child answer the phone? How should they answer the phone? Do you care how your towels are folded? What goes into the hamper? What are your arrangements for doing laundry?

Where do you keep your razors and blades and what rules apply to dangerous bathroom supplies? What brands of soap, shampoo, toothpaste or talc do you purchase?

Remember allergies when choosing toiletries.

KITCHEN AND FOOD RULES

Children often like to be very domestic in their daddy's house. Not only do they feel responsible for taking care of you, they also want to feel that they can fill the void in your life. Decide how much they can do in the kitchen. You should encourage the older children to cook and prepare meals, and to clean up afterwards.

Doing any kitchen chores together makes them easier and fun. Plan who sets or clears the table.

Use paper plates to make the cleanup faster. What will be your rules for washing, wiping, or stacking dishes? If you have a dishwasher, do you rinse before loading the dishes? How often is it turned on? Emptied? Who puts the dishes away?

Who may turn the stove, oven, toaster-oven, and microwave on and off?

Make sure that all pot handles are turned inward when the pots are on the stove. A baby grabbing at a handle or an adult accidentally knocking over a hot pot can cause a horrible accident.

Run cold water or ice water over a burn. Do not put butter or oil on a burn.

Is everything in the refrigerator available for anyone to eat? How will you handle left-overs? How do you feel about eating everything on the plate?

Do you keep vitamins in the kitchen? Who dispenses them? Are they in a safe place?

Who is allowed to sweep? How about washing the floor? Do you wipe the stove top after each time you cook? When do you clean the oven? How do you control bugs?

BEDROOM RULES

What are the sleeping hours? Can they vary? Do you tell bedtime stories? What will be the rules for putting clothes in the hamper or hanging clothes up?

How about putting toys away before bedtime?

Do you sleep with windows open or closed? How about doors? Can the children have a night light? What's the rule on reading in bed?

Does everyone wear robes and slippers or must they get dressed as soon as they get up?

RULES FOR THE LIVING ROOM OR FAMILY ROOM

Are toys allowed in the living room? Is eating allowed in the living room or family room? What is the TV schedule? Who cleans up? Children, even young ones, can dust and vacuum--but don't expect perfection. Do you puff up the pillows on the couch? Do you leave your blinds or shades open or closed?

RULES FOR TRAVELING

Do you create a time schedule for trips? How close do you keep to the schedule? Who sits where in the car? What kind of rules have you set up beforehand to prevent a child from getting lost? What do they do if they do become lost?

Do you introduce games for long trips? Do you remember to use the rules that have been set about food, drink, and bathroom stops? Do you rest and eat properly yourself on trips?

Remember also to be sure that you can describe and identify the children if they get separated. Carry a current picture of the children in the glove compartment. Take your first aid kit on trips.

Do you make sure that everyone in the car wears a seat-belt? Do you have a safe car seat for a young child?

Do you travel with windows open or closed? Do you have an extra key with you when you travel?

TELEPHONE RULES

There is a good chance that your telephone or telephone system is different from the one the children are used to. Make sure they know how to use your phone. Post copies of the emergency numbers you have prepared near each phone in your house. Be sure to have paper and pencil handy, too. Teach them the correct way to respond to a call and how to take messages, and particularly how much information they can give a caller.

If necessary, remind the children to call their mother when they arrive at your home. You'll appreciate getting her support when you are waiting for a call from them.

Establish very specific phone rules for teenagers. Decide on the maximum length of time for calls. If you live a distance from their mother's house, be sure that they realize that calling friends near her home may be long distance from your house.

DISCIPLINE

Along with rules comes punishment for not complying. Punishment is not meant as retaliation --it is a reminder that certain actions are not correct or acceptable. In no way should a child be physically abused.

Think back to your childhood. Don't repeat the kind of punishment that you hated when you were a child. No matter how naughty or destructive a child has been, they should not be deprived of food, sleep, or good care.

Make sure that the child knows that you love him--that it was his action that was bad. Be clear about what was wrong or naughty. Don't punish a child for something they don't know about or understand.

One of the reasons for this very long list of ideas for rules is so that you can establish what is correct behavior and let the child participate in the decision-making.

Decide with the child what the punishment will be for any action long before it becomes an issue. Will you rescind a privilege like watching TV, or going out for an ice cream sundae? Will you discuss the misbehavior?

Think about these decisions when you are cool and the problem has not yet occurred.

ALLOWANCES

If you plan to give the children an allowance, will you give it to them in person when they come to you or as they are leaving for home? Some fathers mail the children's allowances when they mail the support check to their mother.

Help the children design a budget including expenses for birthday and anniversary cards for your family members. There's a good chance they won't get money for those purchases from their mother.

Be fair about recognizing the difference in financial needs of children of different ages.

If you take the time to establish house rules, and the decision-making takes place before conflicts arise, you can reduce the majority of the stress that can occur in day-to-day living.

It is perfectly all right for the rules in your home to be quite different from the rules in their mother's house, as long as the rules are safe, healthy, and make sense. Children do not have trouble with clear, concise, easily-understood decisions. Problems arise when they have to deal with nonexistent directions or wishy-washy permissiveness that changes to harsh reactions under adverse conditions.

If everything is predictable and consistent, there is no reason why the children can't follow the rules. This doesn't mean they will, just that they can. Remember. this second household is still very strange and they are not used to it, or seeing you in it.

Possessions

One of the areas that has to be defined with the children is possessiveness and possessions. In some families there is an "It's mine, and no one can touch it!" rule, and in others, it's "Share and share alike." Decide which rule will guide your family when they are at your house, and then abide by it.

The important aspect of this kind of decision is that it must work both ways. If your family has a "Hands off other people's possessions" policy, that means that your big son cannot borrow your sweater without permission. But it also means that you can't look for it in his dresser drawer.

YOUR PRIVACY

Establish immediately whether dresser drawers, cabinets or closets are private. As an adult with adult habits and privileges, you may have objects and materials around the house that are not suitable for children. Keep them where the children can't find them. Explaining what these things are to an inquisitive child will be much harder than just storing them away where the child can't find them.

THEIR POSSESSIONS

The easiest way to help the children feel that your home is their home is to make some part of our house theirs. If you have been able to rent an apartment with an extra room, let the children have a sizeable part in decorating it (as mentioned in Chapter 5).

Even a very young child can make decisions between the specific choices that you offer. If you can manage the time to make more than one trip to the department and furniture stores, go on a shopping trip alone first. Check prices, colors, availability, and design. Decide what you like and then bring the child to choose between the two, or at most three, items you most prefer.

If you are buying furniture at tag or garage sales, let your children help clean or paint the furniture.

Children can even help make choices about rugs, couches, dishes, and pictures. If you have more than one child, you will have to decide ahead of time if the decisions will be made by majority rule or alternately, one choice per child.

If the children don't have a room of their own, it will be necessary to make something or someplace their special place.

If you have a spare closet, dresser, chest, cabinet, or even dresser drawer, make it theirs. Store the children's clothes and belongings in their special place. If you have a closet, store their cots in it. Hang pictures and art work on the back of the closet door. You might want to purchase a set of underwear, socks, pajamas, slippers, a sweater, a shirt, and jeans to keep at your house in the children's storage place.

If there is absolutely no room at all, plan to save enough space in your closet for a cardboard carton or a plastic "Milkbox." Give each child a grocery bag or a shoebox to decorate in which to store some of their belongings. (See the "Crafts, Activities, and Making Things" section for ideas.) Let the children keep a change of underwear and pajamas and their comb and toothbrush in their bags. Store all the children's bags in the carton box. If you do craft projects, you can also store those materials in the box.

When your children come to visit, pull the box out of the closet so that it is available to them. Make it obvious that they have belongings in your house.

A PLACE FOR EVERYTHING

One of the most frustrating chores that a person can have is keeping a house in order. The most sensible, yet, somehow the most difficult way to maintain order is to put things back right away. Allow the children to help on the weekends, but don't save the whole job for them. If you plan all the housework for Saturday and Sunday, you will just feel that you have a weekend job.

Set up a simple clearing and cleaning schedule for yourself. Do certain chores every day. Save others for specific nights. For instance, a good place to start the cleanup is in the kitchen after supper. Do the supper dishes and pots. Wash the sink and stove and table top. Toss paper plates and garbage in the trash receptacle. Put everything away in its place in the cabinets and drawers. Do a fast sweep up of crumbs and empty the garbage.

Before going to bed, pick up things left around the living room. Empty ashtrays, stack newspapers, put books on their shelves. Plump up pillows. If you snack in the living room, dump any left-overs.

Save the bedroom for the morning. When you get up, straighten the bedding and cover the bed or close the sleeping couch. Put all soiled clothes in the hamper or laundry basket. Hang up what you wore the day before.

Do the bathroom in the morning, too. Clean the mirror after it fogs up, and wash out the sink. Every few days or whenever it needs it, pour some toilet bowl cleaner into the commode. Wipe the tub or shower clean right after use.

Plan to do one larger cleaning chore each night. For instance, vacuum on Monday nights. On Tuesdays and Fridays, dust furniture and empty waste baskets. On Wednesdays, wash the kitchen floor and on Thursdays, do the laundry.

Teach the children to maintain the neat look by doing their share on the weekends.

-+-

Grandparents

When you and your wife divorced, not only did you and your childrens' lives change, but your parents' and your family's lives were affected as well. Very often both husband and wife overlook how much the divorce distresses their parents--the children's grandparents.

VISITING GRANDPARENTS

Some divorce decrees specify guaranteed grandparent visits. Others clearly define the extent and length of visits with grandparents. Because it is often necessary for the children to travel very long distances to see their grandparents, arrangements are often made to consider grandparent visits separately from regular father visitation rights.

However, most frequently, trips to the father's parents have to be arranged within the father's time with the children. After determining your situation, make plans to have the children visit your parents frequently, but with some guidelines.

Often a father lives around the corner from his parents, or even lives with them. If you have that arrangement, be careful to maintain your integrity as your children's father. Don't just pick up the kids and then drop them off at your folks for them to take care of. If you do, you will erode your role as parent, and you might find that you and your own children are being treated as peers by your parents.

If your mother and father live nearby, do make arrangements to have the children visit with them frequently. However, do not plan these grandparent visits for every single time you see the children. Don't relinquish some private time alone with your children.

Arrange the visits to your parents together with the grandparents and the children. Plan that some of the visits with the grandparents occur at your home, or include them in excursions that you make.

RULES FOR THE GRANDPARENTS

It is important to establish ahead of time with your folks exactly how involved they can be in helping you raise your children. It will be necessary to let them know if they may discipline a child, how, in what circumstances, and to what degree. Can they countermand a decision that you have made? Can they change your plans? It is important to make your decisions known--they cannot guess how you feel about these sensitive areas unless you discuss them ahead of time.

Very frequently, grandparents will try to question the children. They feel protective of their own child, you. Because they often want to ensure themselves that the divorce was a good idea, and not your fault, they will ask your kids pointed questions about the children's mother, her social and sex life, how well they are eating, how much they know about the divorce, or even the situations leading up to the divorce. Stop them! Not only are these questions none of their business, but it will antagonize the children.

Undoubtedly, the divorce has left your children with ambivalent feelings about family relationships, and it may be a long time before the children stop feeling that they have to protect each parent from the other. When your parents probe and spy, the children feel that everyone is ganging up on the other parent. This feeling of stress is very difficult for them to deal with, and they may shy away from future visits with your folks. Warn the rest of your family about questioning and prying. Very often an inquisitive or unthinking in-law can create an environment that turns the children against family visits.

Some families get angry at the children for choosing to live with their mother. Don't let anyone punish the children for your unhappiness. Don't let anyone in the family exclude the children from family affairs because of your divorce. And, if there are family events that the children are unable to attend, don't allow your family to hold that against them or you.

When the time comes that you are socializing and getting involved with new relationships, don't let your family press your children for information in that area, either.

It is important to make sure that your parents realize that your divorce has not affected the age or mental powers of the children. Some grandparents scoop up their grandchildren and croon or moan to them, while babbling baby talk, figuring that this will soothe and comfort them. Help your folks remember that these are the same children that they were before the divorce, and the best way to help your kids is to treat them as well as they have in the past. As a matter of fact, the less change the better.

7

THE COOKING BOOK

Mealtime can be fun or it can be an awful chore.

Preparation and cleanup at mealtime can take hours, while the eating part can often be completed in less than 20 minutes. The best advice that can be given is: Try to keep a balance between planning, cooking, eating, and clearing.

Children like simple and recognizable foods. They enjoy talking at a meal, but they rarely can manage lingering at the table for quiet conversation. It is always a good idea to reinforce good table manners in preparation for trips to restaurants, but it is not a good idea to harangue or argue at the table.

Many different kinds of cookbooks are sold in bookstores, supermarkets, discount, department, and specialty stores. The public library has a shelf of cookbooks. Examine a sampling, and after looking them over, buy one or two for yourself. When choosing a cookbook, read several of the recipes. Check to see if the recipe listing contains ingredient names that sound familiar. See if the recipes are easy to read and understand.

The following collection of ideas contains some basic information on quantities and measurements, and terms used in cooking. Some home-spun recipes for leftovers and fun food are included as well.

In the Kitchen

Planning a meal is a great deal like setting up a science experiment. First, you read the instructions, or if you already know the instructions, you review them mentally. Then, you gather all the components or ingredients, and all the equipment you will need to complete the effort. Next, you measure or prepare (pare, slice, open cans, scrub potatoes, etc.) all the ingredients so that they are ready for use. Return the original containers of ingredients to the pantry or storage area, so that you can have as much working room as possible.

Review again to make sure everything is ready. Then, figure the time necessary to complete the actual mixing and cooking of each segment of the meal. Don't forget to include the time needed to preheat the oven. Decide at what time the meal will be served, and then start the part of the meal that takes the longest, first.

Measuring Up

Our great grandmas often cooked by handfuls and pinches, but cookbooks today use specific instructions for quantities. Most American cookbooks use pounds (Lbs.), cups, teaspoons (tsp.), and tablespoons (Tbls.) as standard measurement.

When you buy measuring utensils, you will find that the teaspoon/ tablespoon measure usually has four spoons of various sizes. Along with the two mentioned, there is also a half and a quarter-teaspoon size.

Most spoons are constructed so that they can be inserted in the small metal cans so frequently used for spices. To get a level spoonful of spice, fill the appropriate spoon with the spice and as you remove the spoon, scrape the top along the straight edge of the cutout in the spice can. Another way is to fill a measuring spoon full of the dry ingredient or fat such as butter or shortening and scrap it level with the straight back of a table knife.

Measuring cups come in various sizes and shapes. It is very handy to have a one- or two-quart glass measuring container and a set of individual pre-measured cups. These come in one-cup, half-cup, quarter-cup, and third-cup sizes. These can be used like the measuring spoons. Dip the whole cup into a container of flour or cornmeal or other dry ingredient and scrape it level with the knife.

The easiest way to measure fat is to use the quart-sized glass container. Fill it with water to a mark that is convenient for measuring water displacement. For instance, if you need 1/3 cup of shortening, fill the water to the 2/3 cup mark. Add the fat, or butter until the water hits the 1 cup mark. You can then pour off the water and use the measured butter.

When using a measuring device for liquids, always place the measure so that the cup markings are at eye level.

Additional Measures

Here are some handy, measuring shortcuts for using in recipes:

1/4 pound stick of butter	=	1/2 cup
1/4 pound stick of butter	=	8 Tablespoons
1 cup raisins	=	6 ounces
Juice of one lemon	=	3 Tablespoons
3 teaspoons	=	1 Tablespoon
Tsp.	=	teaspoon
Tbls.	=	tablespoon
4 Tbls.	=	1/4 cup
2 cups	=	1 pint
4 cups or 2 pints	=	1 quart
4 quarts	=	1 gallon
1 pound of sugar	=	2 cups
1 pound brown sugar	=	2 1/4 cups

Frequently Used Cooking Terms

There are several commonly used terms that describe the specific way food is prepared or cooked:

BAKING

Baking is cooking in the top part of the oven. The temperature is usually 350°-450° F. Preheat the oven 8-10 minutes at the correct temperature before inserting the food to be baked into the oven.

Foods that are usually baked are: bread, rolls, biscuits, pies, and cookies. Scrubbed white potatoes, sweet potatoes, and large squash can be baked in the oven. Pierce the potato skins a few times. Bake for an hour at 400° F. in a regular oven or 8 minutes in a microwave. Slice large squash (like Hubbard) and remove the seeds. Place the squash into a deep glass baking dish or a pan and dot the slices with butter. Pour a little honey or pancake syrup on the squash. Bake it for about 45 minutes to 1 hour at 350° F.

BOILING

Boiling is the term used for cooking in boiling water. Boiling water has large, briskly breaking bubbles. Food is introduced into the boiling water, and if it is being timed, the timing starts when the water returns to the boiling state.

Water is brought to the boiling point before hard-cooking eggs or simmering vegetables. Spaghetti and pasta, and some vegetables, are boiled.

To make spaghetti and macaroni, put 1 tsp. salt and 1/2 tsp. of oil or butter into a deep pot containing 2-3 quarts of rapidly boiling water. Add the spaghetti or macaroni and stir until it is submerged under water. Time the boiling for 8 minutes from the time it returns to a brisk boil, stirring occasionally. Test one strand or noodle to see if it is soft enough. Check every 2-3 minutes. Don't let spaghetti overcook. Drain in a colander, and then serve with melted butter, spaghetti sauce, canned clam sauce, or grated parmesan cheese.

FRYING

Frying is cooking in hot fat in a shallow frying pan. If you want to cut down on calories use as little fat as possible. You can also purchase a pan-coating material (for instance, PAM(c)) that doesn't add calories to the food, but prevents food from sticking to the pan.

Eggs can be fried, and so can meat, fish, fowl, and potatoes.

DEEP FRYING

When you deep fry, food is totally covered by hot fat and is cooked in a deep pot or fryer. Drain fried foods on paper toweling before serving to get rid of the greasy look.

Doughnuts, french fries, and chicken can be deep-fried.

BROILING AND GRILLING

When food is broiled, it is in direct contact with heat or fire. Broiling is done in the bottom of the oven, under a flame or electric coil. You can raise or lower the grilling pan slightly. Use your own pan with a rack in it, right inside the oven pan (minus its rack). It is usually easier to wash than the oven rack and pan, or you can line the oven pan with aluminum foil and spray the rack with PAM to make the job easier. Grilling is done on a grill, barbecue, or hibachi. The flame is under the food. Grills <u>must</u> be used out doors.

Grilling is an excellent way to make steaks, chops, fish, or chicken breasts on a rib bone. Broil meat that is no more than 1 1/2-2 inches thick.

To broil fish, arrange the cleaned whole fish, skin-side down or place fillets in a buttered or greased pan. Season with salt, pepper, and herbs such as basil, marjoram, savory, or thyme. Sprinkle with lemon juice and dot with butter. Baste occasionally. Fish is ready when it is white (pink for salmon), firm, and flakes easily.

STEWING

Stewing is the process of cooking slowly in a little liquid in a covered pot. Any stew recipe can be started in the morning in a crock pot and be ready for dinner when you come home from work.

You can make homemade soups the same way as stew, just using more water. Lamb and beef stews are particularly tasty, and chili is also cooked like stew.

ROASTING

You are roasting when you cook food uncovered in an oven. When you roast or bake, preheat the oven for 8-10 minutes before inserting the food to be cooked.

You can roast beef, lamb, pork, chicken or turkey. Get a meat thermometer that inserts into the thickest part of the meat or fowl that you are cooking so you can gauge when your meal is thoroughly cooked.

Check the temperature guide on the meat thermometer before inserting it in the meat and then check the thermometer reading when you baste.

Internal Temperature
of Meat When Properly Cooked

Rare beef................ 140°
Ham .... 160°

Medium beef.............. 160°
Well done beef........... 170°
Pork..................... 170°
Veal..................... 170°
Lamb..................... 180°
Poultry.................. 185°

Roast meat or poultry in a deep pan (a roaster). Baste the meat frequently (about every 1/3-3/4 hour) using pan drippings to keep the food moist, and to give it a nicely browned surface.

Most meats roast at 325-350° F. To prepare the meat, just pat it dry with paper toweling. Season with a moderate amount of salt, pepper, and any combination of two or three of the following herbs: basil, marjoram, oregano, rosemary, savory, or thyme. Sprinkle the spices and herbs on the surface and rub into the meat.

General Time Guide for Roasting

325 — 350° F

Beef Rare	15 minutes/lb.
Beef Medium	20 minutes/lb.

Beef Well Done	30 minutes/lb.
4-6 Lb. Beef Rib Roast	35-38 minutes/lb.
3-5 Lb. Pork Loin	30-35 minutes/lb.
5-7 Lb. fully cooked boneless ham	18-24 minutes/lb.
4 Lb. Chicken	20-30 minutes/lb.

SIMMERING

Simmering means to cook just below the boiling point.

Soups, some vegetables, and cooked fruit are simmered.

To heat canned vegetables, just open the can, pour them into a small pot, heat to almost boiling, and then serve.

For frozen vegetables, bring just an inch or two of water (to which you may add 1/4 tsp. salt) to a boil. Add the vegetables. Let the water return to a boil and then lower the flame. Allow the vegetables to continue simmering for the period of time stated on the package. Note that corn-on-the-cob needs more water than does small vegetables or vegetable pieces.

Fresh vegetables can be served raw or cooked. Peel, pare, or scrape the skins off root vegetables. Cut large vegetables into small pieces. Cook them like frozen vegetables. Check after 8-10 minutes, testing for tenderness. Allow vegetables to simmer until tender but still slightly crisp. Carrots, turnips, and potatoes take longer.

DREDGING

Dredging is to coat lightly with flour. For example, meat is often coated with flour before braising, browning, or sauteing.

BRAISING

Braising is browning meat in a little fat in a frying pan, before cooking another way. Stew meat is usually braised first.

BASTING

Basting is done to keep food from drying while roasting. Use gravy, soup, or liquid to frequently moisten the food. Use a soup ladle or a gravy spoon to lift liquid from a deep pot.

DICING

To dice food, cut it into small cubes. Cut vegetables into large circular slices, and then make parallel cuts across the slices. Turn 180 degrees and slice across the previously made cuts. If you don't have a cutting board, work on a folded sheet of wax paper.

PARING

Paring is often called peeling because you are removing the peel or skin. If you have a garbage disposal, you can throw orange or lemon peelings plus a few ice cubes into the disposal and turn it on. This trick makes the disposal and the kitchen smell great.

Using Leftovers

If you have a microwave oven, you can reheat a meal without drying the food. As a result, you can cook a large portion and freeze or refrigerate part of it for future meals. Prepare separate meal-size portions on the plastic microwave plates saved from commercial frozen food dinners.

You can use leftovers in many ways that are different from their original use. Imagination and your memory of tastes and flavors will help you think of unusual ways. You might try some of the following:

BAKED LEFTOVER MASHED POTATOES

Mix a little butter and finely diced or grated cheese into mashed potatoes. Place the potatoes in a glass pie plate for the microwave or an aluminum foil pan for the conventional oven, and spread out evenly. Sprinkle with paprika, dot with butter (arranging tiny bits of butter all over the surface), and bake until top is delicately brown.

FRIED MASHED POTATO CAKES

Mix 2-3 cups of mashed potatoes with one beaten egg and desired seasonings such as salt, pepper, or garlic salt. Wet your hands with cold water and form golf ball sized balls. Put 1/2 cup flour in a small bowl. (You may need some more as you work.) Put a potato ball in the flour and flatten it. Turn it over so that both sides are dredged with flour. When they are all ready, fry them gently in a little fat or oil.

STUFFED RE-BAKED POTATOES

Slice baked potatoes in half along their length. Scoop out the potato skins and mash the potatoes you have removed, adding milk and butter. Pile the mashed potatoes back into the skins and bake until lightly browned.

HOME FRIES OR COTTAGE FRIES

Slice or dice cold leftover baked potatoes and fry gently in a little oil. They are especially good if diced or sliced onion and/or green pepper is fried along with them.

VARIOUS LEFTOVER VEGETABLES

After completing dinner, pour any leftover vegetables into a large jar, and store it in the freezer. Keep adding successive leftover vegetables to the jar.

Mix two or three leftover cooked vegetables with different colors or textures (like sliced carrots, broccoli and green beans) to make a vegetable medley. Heat and serve.

Another use for leftover vegetables is for making a country-style soup. To make the soup, add some of the vegetables from the jar of frozen leftovers to a pot of boiling beef broth, chicken broth, or consomme (canned) made using the instructions on the can. Add leftover meat to the meat soups, or leftover chicken to the chicken-based soup. Lower the heat so that the soup simmers. Allow it to cook for a half hour to an hour. Serve it with Italian or French bread for a winter weekend lunch.

RICE PILAF

Add a vegetable medley (as above) to leftover rice to make a rice pilaf. Warm the rice and vegetable mix in the microwave or add a few drops of water and warm it in a covered pot on the stove.

If your pot doesn't have a cover, use a plate as a lid. Remove the plate very cautiously, using an oven mitt.

CHINESE STYLE FRIED RICE

Heat a small amount of oil in a frying pan. Break an egg over the hot oil and stir it rapidly until it looks like stringy scrambled eggs. Add the rice pilaf described above. Sprinkle some soy sauce over the rice and stir. Small pieces of chicken, meat, or shrimp can be added to Fried Rice.

LEFTOVER COOKED HAMBURGER

When you make more hamburgers than you and the kids can eat, put the uneaten portions in the freezer. Heat them in the microwave for a quick supper.

You can also break the cold, cooked hamburger into small pieces and warm it in commercially prepared barbecue sauce. Serve on bread or bun as "Sloppy Joes."

LEFTOVER RAW HAMBURGER MEAT--
Spaghetti Sauce with Meat

Heat a small amount of oil in a frying pan. Add the hamburger meat, breaking it into tiny pieces with a fork. Stir the meat until all of it is browned and then pour off the fat. Add a large can or two small cans of tomato sauce, a teaspoon each of oregano, basil, and parsley, and 1/2 tsp. garlic powder (or instead, use a jar of prepared spaghetti sauce.) Stir and then allow the sauce to simmer for 10 minutes. Pour it over hot spaghetti or macaroni.

CHICKEN OR TURKEY A LA KING

Heat a can of cream of mushroom soup just as it comes from the can (without adding any liquid) on a low flame. Add leftover cooked chicken or turkey that has been cut into small pieces. Pour over biscuits or toast. Try adding leftover green peas to the soup and chicken.

CHICKEN OR TURKEY SALAD

Dice cold leftover cooked chicken or turkey. Chop a stalk of celery (do not include the leaves) and a small onion, and add to the chicken. Season and mix in a tablespoon of mayonnaise or salad dressing. Add more mayo if necessary. A tasty addition is chopped apple, grapes, and/or walnuts.

LEFTOVER SLICED BEEF, PORK, OR TURKEY--
Hot Open-Faced Sandwiches

Make a packet of beef, pork, or turkey gravy as instructed on the back of the package or open and heat a can of gravy. Lay the meat on bread or toast and arrange it on a plate. Pour hot gravy over it to make a hot open-faced sandwich.

SPICY LEFTOVER MEATLOAF

Pour barbecue sauce or ketchup into a frying pan, so that it covers the bottom. Add slices of cold leftover meatloaf. Heat until the meat is coated and heated through. The pan gets messy but the dinner is great.

SPARKLING MIXED JUICE DRINK

Mix leftover fruit juices together, add ginger ale, and pour over ice.

FRUIT

Make a different dessert with leftover canned fruit. Pour the fruit (without juice) over pound cake or sponge cake. Top with whipped cream.

Or to make a fruit compote, mix small pieces of fresh fruit with leftover canned fruit, and then serve the fruit in another fruit that is hollow, like a melon half.

You can also stir canned fruit into prepared gelatin dessert, like Jello(R), which has cooled but not set.

Check the gelatin box for instructions about pineapple.

COFFEE OR TEA

Use leftover coffee or tea for making ice cubes for summer drinks. Using coffee ice cubes in iced coffee or coffee flavored liquer drinks prevents them from becoming diluted.

BLENDED DRINKS

Add cold coffee or fruits (like peaches, strawberries or bananas) and a little plain ice cream to milk. Use a blender to stir into a cool drink.

EGG WHITES--
Baked Alaska

You can make a very elegant dessert very easily. Beat 4-6 egg whites until they are very stiff. Egg whites will only beat stiffly if there is nothing foreign in them, so be careful not to get any yolk in the white. When you lift the beaters, the beaten egg whites should peak and stay. Add 4-6 tablespoons of confectioner's sugar, which is soft, almost like flour, while you continue beating the eggs. Add 1/4 teaspoon of vanilla extract.

Heap the beaten egg whites over ice cream on sliced sponge or pound cake. Cover every bit of the ice cream and cake with the beaten egg whites. Put the dessert under the broiler of a regular oven, about four inches below the heat. Brown quickly and serve immediately. You can add a cherry to the top of the dessert after removing it from the oven or even pour brandy over the top.

Fun Foods To Make With Children

The following suggestions for fun foods turn ordinary food into something special. The nutrition remains the same--they are just served differently.

EGGS AND TOAST DISHES

Egyptian Eye

Try these ideas for different breakfasts. Crack an egg and pour it into a small bowl. Cut the center out of a slice of bread. (You can use an inverted juice glass to cut a perfect circle.) Heat a small frying pan and melt a tablespoon of butter in the pan. Lightly fry the square slice of bread minus the circle. Turn it over when it gets brown. When the second side is almost brown, pour the egg into the center hole. Let the egg cook through. Turn over very gently and then serve.

Scrambled Eggs in the Nest

Remove crusts from as many slices of white bread as there are people to feed. Butter both sides of the bread and press into muffin-pan cups. Preheat the oven to 325° F. Bake the bread 20-25 minutes or until it is golden brown. Remove the toast cups from the oven. Prepare scrambled eggs. Fill the cups with the cooked eggs. Serve with bacon or ham.

HAPPY PANCAKES

Prepare pancake batter as described on the

pancake mix package. On a hot griddle or frying pan, pour small circles of batter instead of large ones. These will be eyes. Pour a frankfurter shape to make a clown smile. Arrange the parts on a plate like a face. Make a pat of butter the nose.

You could also use a slice of bacon for the smile or a strawberry for a nose.

ANIMAL PANCAKES

Pour pancake batter so that it forms a large circle or oval. Add small circles or pancake batter to the edge of the big pancake for the head, feet, and tail. Turtles and bunnies are especially easy pancake animals.

TOAST ANIMALS

Use animal shape cookie cutters to cut animals out of white bread slices. Toast in a pan with a little butter. Serve with cooked cereal that you sprinkle with brown sugar.

FRENCH TOAST

Dip bread slices into two beaten eggs that have been mixed with 1/2 cup milk. Delicately fry in a little butter.

French toast, pancakes, or waffles can be served with either warm or cold syrup, jam, jelly, marmalade, honey, or brown sugar, confectioner's sugar, or cinnamon and sugar.

SURPRISE HAMBURGERS

You might try the following for a lunch or a supper time meal.

One pound of ground beef can make four large Surprise Hamburgers. Divide the meat into eight equal portions. Wet your hands with cold water and roll each portion into a ball, and then press it quite flat. Heat a frying pan, and then add a sprinkling of salt to it. Place all eight burgers into the pan to brown. Turn four burgers over and put one or more of the following on the center of the browned side: a cube of cheese, a pickle slice, 1 tsp. relish. Top each filled half with a plain burger half, browned sides facing. Press together, and then turn to brown the last side.

STUFFED FRANKFURTERS

Broil frankfurters, turning frequently, until all sides are glistening. Remove the franks from the broiler and cut a slit in them the long way down the center. Fill the slit with cheese, relish, and mustard or ketchup. Return the franks to the broiler to melt the cheese.

SILLY SANDWICHES

Discovering a strange and unexpected filling

in a frankfurter roll is what makes these sandwiches "silly."

Fill toasted frankfurter rolls with tuna, chicken or turkey salad instead of frankfurters.

SANDWICH BOATS

Add a sail made of paper mounted on a toothpick to sandwiches served in a frankfurter roll. Sail them on a "sea" of lettuce.

MELTED CHEESE SANDWICHES

Lightly toast a slice of bread in the broiler. Remove it from the stove and butter it. Cover with a slice of cheese and return to the broiler. Heat just until the cheese melts.

You can add a slice or two of cooked bacon under or on top of the cheese. Try a slice of boiled ham or cooked asparagus under the cheese.

FANCY CHICKEN WINGS OR LEGS

Buy a package of frozen chicken wings or legs that are covered with batter and pre-cooked. (They may be in the party section of the freezer.) Cook them for one-third the time recommended on the package. Drizzle honey, and sesame seeds over the heated chicken. Turn the pieces over so that all sides are covered and return them to the oven for the remainder of the suggested cooking time.

FRUIT SALADS AND DESSERTS

Fruits, and fruit and vegetable combinations, make appealing salads. Serve them on a bed of lettuce.

Mix chopped or grated carrots and raisins moistened with mayo or salad dressing.

Fill peach or apricot halves with cottage cheese.

Mix segments or slices of fresh fruit together. Serve with plain or animal cookies.

Make fruit animals and serve as a salad or a dessert. Use a canned pear half for a bunny body. Add a small marshmallow for a tail and two almonds for ears.

Turn a peach half into a turtle. Use a cherry or grape for a head and nut pieces for the feet and tail.

A peach half can be decorated with raisins to look like a pumpkin for a Halloween salad.

When the circus comes to town, celebrate by making a peach or pear clown. Use pimento for a mouth, raisins for eyes, and a small marshmallow or cherry for a nose. Make the peach look even more like a clown by creating a whip cream collar.

You can also turn a peach into a duck by using a marshmallow or round shaped fruit for a head. Use two almonds for the beak and a raisin for the eye.

COOKIES

You can make freshly baked cookies easily without doing any mixing. Tubes of sugar cookie dough, oatmeal cookie dough, and chocolate-chip cookie dough are available in the dairy case of the supermarket. Just follow the instructions for the correct oven temperature and baking time.

To make animal cookies, allow a tube of sugar cookie dough to soften and then roll out small amounts of dough. If you don't have a rolling pin, cover a can of beans or vegetables or cover a broom stick, with aluminum foil and use it for rolling the dough 1/4 inch thick. Cover your work surface with wax paper. Use animal shape cutters or make shapes of cardboard and cut around them.

Bake the cookies using the directions on the package.

-+-

The kitchen has always been the heart of a home and the place where much family interaction takes place. Make the time you spend in the kitchen fun.

If you include the children in the preparation of meals, even the most finicky eater responds more positively. Allow the children to show off some of their cooking skills on occasion, but do insist that everyone participates in cleanup.

Take allergies and food reactions into consideration when making food purchases. You can make alternative choices in foods while still maintaining good nutrition. Avoid, if possible, packaged goods with artificial coloring, flavorings, or preservatives. Natural foods are healthier and safer, and there are many choices on the food shelves.

Enjoy your kitchen and your home. You will find that your life is much more relaxed when you don't have to keep taking children to restaurants, and you will discover that eating at home is also much more economical.

8

THE OUTSIDE WORLD

By now you have surely discovered that your life is very different than it was when you were married. You may be very confused, feel somewhat lost, or feel depressed. You may have discovered a re-alignment of friends and relations. Many of your best friends may be disappearing out of your life just when you need them the most, while others may offer to share a lifestyle which you are not interested in nor even feel comfortable with.

Some of your acquaintances or associates might make light of your situation, while others might want to delve deeply into your psyche--and share their insights into your life and your future. Your extended family probably has started treating you differently, and your parents are also probably worried about you. You are probably broke too, and surely your children are acting differently.

Start to regain control of your life by realizing that there were problems in your life before the divorce and there are going to be problems in your new life. The problems that occur in adult lives--illness, lack of money, loneliness, guilt, concern, sexual frustration, lack of time, new social conditions, work-associated problems, loss of friends, disinterested relatives, overly-interested relatives, social pressures, religious pressures, and so on--will all reflect on your relationships with the children. Bear in mind that the newly-divorced have all or most of these problems. Some are solved quickly with ease, some solve themselves and many are going to be alleviated with time, if you allow that to happen.

Help With Your Problems

Your children are going to be a large source of your new problems for a period of time after the divorce. Their entire lives have been changed and they don't have the experience to cope with these changes. They are going to carry stress back and forth from their mother's house to yours and then back to hers again to test their new environments. They have to learn, very quickly, how to deal with their new lives. They can cause problems, and be problems.

They can become very manipulative, accusing you of making their mother unhappy, and accusing her of causing you grief. One of the quickest ways to nip this kind of behavior in the bud is to insist that you don't want stories carried back and forth. Even if your curiosity is killing you, don't ask personal questions about their mother's life and insist that what goes on in your home is private.

They recognize that both you and your former wife are going through severe stress and a readjustment period. Your kids can tell when you are both unsure of your footing, and then they take advantage. They might very possibly ask for all sorts of privileges and gifts. You cannot fix unhappiness with presents--don't give in to this form of manipulation. But do try to enhance their lives by reassuring them that you are still their father, that you love them, and that in time everyone will be used to this new life and will be happy again.

Children are curious. They want to know all about your new life. They may examine drawers, closets, and book shelves. If you have anything that you don't want them to see (and that includes pay stubs, rent receipts, letters, bills, or reading material), keep them in a locked box and store them where they are not accessible (as mentioned in Chapter 6). This does not suggest that all children are sneaks, but many are completely surprised when their parents announce their divorce, and they don't want to be surprised about anything else ever again.

Another thing about most children--they truly do believe that they are the cause of their parents' divorce. Perhaps it is their childish egos, but many feel that even if they didn't directly cause the divorce by their "bad behavior" or "faults," they could have at least had the power to stop it.

Your children may feel a responsibility for patching up the differences between you and your ex-wife, and for getting you both together again. They try all kinds of games and gimmicks from wishing on stars, to reporting that their mother is ill and needs you. They describe their mother's dates, and tell her about yours. They tell you how beautiful she looks or how sad and miserable she has become. They give your female friends a hard time and do the same to her male friends.

You have to repeat frequently that the divorce is not their fault, that it is permanent, and that you love them. It might even be necessary to differentiate between love for a child and love for a mate, to help them understand that you will not get a divorce from them.

Television and the half-hour format (where a problem arises and is solved in 30 minutes between commercial and station breaks) has been influential in our thinking processes. Life is not that simple. Problems arise and carry over from one visit to the next. Some problems cause others. Some need piece-by-piece unraveling. Others may need the cooperation of your former wife. Be patient. Get professional advice when things become difficult to sort out. There are many agencies that deal with problems just like yours. Look in your phone book, newspaper, or church and synagogue bulletins for other listings. Some agencies or groups might suggest others. The list below is just a start. Jot the telephone number of your local agency next to the name below.

Alcoholics Anonymous
Catholic Charities
Child Abuse Hotline
Child Study Centers
Child Welfare
Community Churches
Community Synagogues
Family Counseling
First Call for Help
Goodwill Agencies
Jewish Social Service Agency
Mental Health Association
National Run-A-Way Hotline
Parenting Guidance Centers
Parents Without Partners
Pastoral Centers
Survivors of Suicide
Teen Challenge
United Way
Urban Ministries
Welfare Department

Single Parent Groups

Join a single-parent organization like Parents Without Partners and participate in their varied activities.

PWP is the means to return to a social existence in a non-threatening way. You will be particularly interested in the discussion groups. No one is forced to participate, but just hearing that other people have or have had the same problems as you makes it easier to deal with, especially when you discover that for many, those problems are in the past. There is an amazing openness and freedom in many of these meetings. All kinds of topics are discussed from behavior problems to first date fears and impotence. And even such sensitive topics as these are handled openly by men and women alike.

Parents Without Partners is an organization of divorced, widowed, and non-married parents. It provides a re-introduction to a social existence as well as support services. The individual members hold card games, language courses, backgammon classes, house parties, ski and vacation trips, play-reading groups, and many other activities. They also provide an atmosphere within which fathers can plan activities for their children. There is usually a specific father's group that arranges activities that include children who have no male parent or male role model with whom to interact.

Attend a discussion group with your children that is made up of other children and teenagers. You will discover a great deal from what they have to say. It may help you solve your children's problems and help them feel that other kids are dealing with the same problems that they have, and that they are not unique.

Your Friends

Once you have started thinking about seeing people again, you very often have to learn the complexities of dating and socializing all over.

There is a definite tendency to try to act younger. You might find that you are changing your clothing style and checking your hairline. You are, after all, re-entering a phase of life usually completed in the late teens. There is nothing wrong with acting younger, as long as you don't try to compete with your children. Don't flaunt your sex life or dating habits.

It's very healthy and helpful to share what's going on in your new life, but don't distress the children by pushing them into making comparisons with their mother. Use activities like those offered by PWP to introduce the children to your new friends in non-threatening group situations.

Your life, which may have become very narrow, will one day soon, start to open up enough to include new friends and relationships. It is true that at first you didn't see how you would ever find new friends or interests, but as time goes on, people at work, old friends, and relatives start introducing new people. You might meet some at singles clubs or bars. A few new people in your life may be friends that you can learn from, while some will be people that you use, or who use you. Others may introduce new and strange life styles.

During this awakening, you may be involved in a certain amount of self-centered activity. Your children can easily become secondary during this exciting period of time--don't allow this to happen.

You find yourself quoting new people and new things. If you are seeing a psychologist or counselor, you have a need to share the things you are learning about yourself. You want to talk about things that you have never talked about before.

For some reason, getting a divorce for many men frees them from the constraints that they have had since they were young. (Perhaps because they married when they themselves were still kids.) But now that you have children of your own, you are going to have to be careful how you act or what you talk about in front of them. Some subjects are too complex and not meant to be casually discussed with children.

Your Special Friend

Eventually the time comes when one person becomes more important and interesting to you than the rest of the people you know. You develop a relationship with some woman with whom you want to spend a great deal of time. She becomes the center of your life and the center of things you want to do.

Be cautious not to steal from the time you usually save for the children. Introduce your lady friend into their scheduled time with moderation. When you do activities or take trips together as a group, make sure that they are geared to the children, not to your friend. Make these together-times infrequent until you know that this lady will be really involved in your life. The children have just gone through the divorce of their parents--the people they thought were going to be together forever. They are not ready for, nor do they understand, temporary relationships. Children get emotionally involved in your life and if the new person in your life doesn't work out, it will be like another divorce for them. So, keep your special person important only to you until you know it's permanent.

If you really love this lady, the children will handle it because they love you. But they are going to compare her to their mother, and they may feel that it is disloyal to like her too quickly. Your lady will have to be very mature and strong until they adjust, and they will need your help and understanding to do that.

Don't involve your children in your sex life. They are not old enough to handle your sexuality, no matter what their age. Don't show off your prowess, even if you have the need to impress someone and stroke your own ego. They don't have to know about your accomplishments.

Don't compete with your teenagers. Their dating is different from yours. There are different physical, emotional, and psychological barriers for adults and teens. Maintain your parenting role and don't color their experiences by comparing them to those of an adult.

Expecting Grownup Behavior From Small Children

Children have simple interests and moderate tastes so when the children are with you, or when you make plans that include them, make the plans fit.

Keep their activities low-key--take them places that are receptive to children or designed specifically for children. Create a framework into which they can fit. Plan your time together to meet their needs and capabilities. You will enjoy their companionship much more when it is without stress.

9

HOLIDAYS AND SPECIAL TIMES

The elements that define a family are the people, the things that the people do, and they ways they interact. Holidays and special occasions are a very important part of what makes a group of people a family. Now, because of the divorce, all the special holidays things that you used to do may have to be done differently.

Decide how you are going to celebrate holidays in your re-defined family unit. Determine which holidays you get to see the children and how long they can stay with you. Then make plans to celebrate the best way you can. Keeping some of the routine of your former life helps you with your own mental health.

If in the past, you always had Christmas or Hanukah at your wife's folks and Thanksgiving at your folks, see if it is possible to continue a similar schedule. Try not to make any big changes until the children are really used to you in your new life. Try to maintain rituals, traditions, and family uniqueness despite the fact that it is occurring in two different homes.

Rituals and Traditions

Although children can learn to accept different house rules, they find it difficult to change the rituals and traditions that establish the framework of their family. Replicate the traditions that have been established in your family. Many will be a blend of your family's ways and those of your former wife's family. Therefore, they can be acceptable to both.

For instance, if the "Tooth Fairy" leaves a dime for a lost tooth under a pillow, don't change to a quarter, when they are with you. Or, if your family always sings Christmas Carols on Christmas Eve and opens presents the next morning, continue the same pattern when they visit you.

For fun, sometime, get into a conversation with several adults and ask how their families celebrate a special holiday. Watch the reactions. People are often surprised by what others do and may even get upset or repelled by the differences. Remember how you and your wife had to adjust to each other's traditions.

Keep the same food traditions, too. If you have always had turkey at Thanksgiving, continue that tradition even if you are eating alone. Get a small frozen turkey roast, or buy turkey portions. Nothing else will taste right. Don't change to goose or venison, now.

Invite other single friends to join you for a holiday when you are not seeing the children. Ask each person coming to provide part of the meal. Spend holidays with other people--don't be alone.

Rituals are based on having an expectation that is handed on from generation to generation, stabilized or enhanced from family to family. It is that heritage that binds people together, connecting their past and their present.

Changes in rituals and traditions can be more upsetting than many of the other (even larger) changes that you make in your life.

School Events

Most of the elementary school activities the children are involved in occur during the day. Therefore, it will probably be difficult to attend. Others are impossible to attend because the school is such a great distance. As a result, many fathers lose contact with their children's schools and school work. Even those dads who were really involved with their kids' school and homework just are not where this is all taking place. Try to attend many of the school events that take place in the evenings. School is a very important part of the children's lives. It takes up as much time in their lives as your work does in yours.

Keep in touch with their school lives the best you can. Attend PTA meetings and open-house. Speak to their teachers and principals. Ask the children to bring you some of the pictures that they drew, papers that they wrote or math problems that they did, when they come to visit. Invite them to do some of their homework when they are at your house.

Just asking to see report cards is not enough--but it is better than nothing.

Special Occasions Also Attended by the Other Parent

There are going to be some occasions that you and your former wife have to attend at the same time. These may be very uncomfortable at first. The school events like concerts or plays will probably be the first ones. When it comes to your children's school activities, graduations, Bar Mitzvahs, engagement parties or weddings, try to arrange to be civil to each other, to sit together, and to share this moment as a group, if not a family.

At other occasions like the weddings, funerals, or graduations of mutual friends or family, you don't have to sit together if you don't want to. Try to make arrangements though, to have the children sit with each of you part of the time. It might be a good idea to put on a facade at these events and act as cordially as possible. It will make the next time easier.

These forced social situations are difficult, but they are going to occur. Handle them as calmly and graciously as possible. In that way, you and the children will suffer the least stress.

Help the children realize that these get-togethers will occur and not to see them as occasions that cause you and your former wife to reconsider getting together.

Your Vacation

You deserve a vacation, and you really do deserve this vacation without the children so that you can go to sophisticated places with adult friends. However, if the only time that you can see the children is during your two weeks of vacation, you'll have to come to terms with the fact that they deserve your time.

That means that you should arrange your vacation so that the children can be entertained by the environment. Theme, water, and wildlife parks, can provide the entertainment for you. In that way, you get the most rest, have a vacation, and still have quality time with the children because you can make the choice to participate or just be a by-stander.

On the other hand, if you take your kids someplace where all the facilities and activities are geared to an adult, you still have to find a way to entertain them. Or you'll have to find someplace within that environment that provides care for the children, and then you will miss spending your time with them.

What If You Can't Make It?

There are going to be times that are scheduled for seeing the children that you won't be able to make because of a business trip, illness, or other emergency. Try to keep these occurrences to an absolute minimum.

If such a situation occurs, let the children know as soon as possible, and let their mother know, too. Don't have the children anticipate your visits until the last minute and then disappoint them. Always let them know personally that you can't make it. Phone them and share what you might do on your next visit. See if you can arrange with their mother to make up the time you have missed.

Send the children a card or letter from wherever you are. Show them that you haven't forgotten them nor have you put them out of your mind just because you are away on a business trip.

Very often a birthday falls on a day of the week that you don't see the child. Even if you will see the child on the weekend (and will personally present your gift), still send a card to arrive on the special day, and try to call. Children remember the special events in their lives as benchmarks. Let the children know that you remember the occasion; you just can't be with them.

Not too far in the future, you will find that the children start to remember to call you on your birthday, and special holidays, too. They'll reciprocate by showing that they care about your feelings, too.

10

THE BABY BOOK/PEOPLE BOOK

The Baby Book/People Book is an idea that is an outgrowth of the familiar baby book. But this one is about all of your children, all of the information you collect about them, and all of your activities. It will help give a family feeling of continuity. You can use any kind of large, blank-paged book like a scrap book or a photo album to create this collection of memories. It is a continuous ongoing story of your children's lives (on their own and with you).

Log of Events

The first thing to keep is a diary of events and activities that take place every visit. Whenever you do anything, just add it to the log. For instance, an entry might be: "On June 6 we went to the wild animal land." "Jimmy took his first photos." Another might be: "On June 7 we made chocolate chip cookies."

The kids can write the list themselves or you can do it for very young children. You can go back to this book anytime and review the experiences and things you have done together. Get some input about the activities from the children. Did they like what they did? Did they love it? Would they do it again? Record their responses next to the entries. It will help guide in making future plans.

The Photo Album

Include photographs in the Baby Book/People Book. It is very nice to take pictures every time something special happens, but if that is not possible, take a picture on birthdays or holidays. Label each picture with the date and the occasion when the picture was taken, and the name and the age of the child. If it is a group picture, label all the people in the group. Make sure there are pictures of you with the children, as well as individual pictures of each child.

Add extra useful information to the annual photograph. For example, you can record the sizes of the children's clothes. Most clothes have a size and laundering label on the neck or waistband. Make a note of shirt, pants, dress, and shoe sizes, and if you want to purchase any clothes, the salesperson can figure the correct size from this information. You can anticipate children's sizes as they get older by figuring that usually children grow one (or two) sizes a year until their teens. Then they grow even more rapidly.

Copies of Records

Another group of items that belong in the Baby Book/People Book are copies of records. It is a good place to keep a copy of important medical records and prescriptions. Keep a copy of birth or baptismal certificates. Keep a record of the children's growth, photocopies of report cards, letters from teachers, and special commendations. Get duplicate newspaper articles in which the children, their schools, or their teams are mentioned.

In the Baby Book/People Book, paste pictures, photographs, and mementos. They will help you examine and review the past with your children. Children love to hear about their childhood and stories about when they were growing up. They love to hear about incidents in their lives, their personal problems, and how they overcame them.

Hearing these stories and looking at tangible reminders in the Baby Book/People Book will give them an understanding of your parenting and will be a guide for their own development of parenting skills.

Now that you have had a chance to make both your new home and your new life the kind that you can truly enjoy with your children, you will probably find that you are beginning to live a full life again. Happy parenting!

To order a copy of Survival Guide for a Weekend Father for a friend, cut the coupon below:

Enclose the coupon and a check or money order for $10.95 plus $2.00 for mailing and handling for:
Survival Guide for a Weekend Father.
Texas residents add 6.25% for tax.

Orcas Press, Inc.
Suite 206
601-2 Harwood Road
Bedford, Tx 76021

Name:______________________________

Address:____________________________

City______________State:___Zip:_____

Enclose the coupon and a check or money order for $10.95 plus $2.00 for mailing and handling for:
Survival Guide for a Weekend Father.
Texas residents add 6.25% for tax.

Orcas Press, Inc.
Suite 206
601-2 Harwood Road
Bedford, Tx 76021

Name:______________________________

Address:____________________________

City______________State:___Zip:_____